From Niagara Falls
to Air Force One
and Back

A Memoir by Jeffrey Elder

© 2021 by Janis F. Kearney

All rights reserved. No part of this book may be reproduced or transmitted in any form or by any means, electronic or mechanical, including photocopying, recording or by any information storage and retrieval system, without permission in writing from the publisher.

Writing Our World Publishing

2 Rosier Court, Little Rock, Arkansas 72211

www.WOWPublishing.org

First Writing Our World Publishing Edition

ISBN: 978-0-9889644-6-4 (Soft Cover)
ISBN: 978-0-578-25017-5 (Hard Cover

Library of Congress Control Number: 2019913947

Printed in the United States of America

Dedication

This book is dedicated to the people I love most
and who have been there for me

Mom Lula & Pops Willie, Vicki, Brianna, Danielle, Gianna & Aiden

As well as those most missed

Granny Lula Mae Elder & Eric Michael Fontaine

and my great friend Glenn W. Powell

Table of Contents

Foreword 9

Introduction 11

Part One: The Love Canal

The Elder Family of Niagara Falls 14

Griffon Manor 17

The Love Canal 21

Born to Travel 23

Finding My Father 30

The Carousel Skate Center 34

On the Cusp of Adulthood 42

Part Two: On Becoming a Man

The Hair Cut 46

An Airman's Story: Coming Home to Leave 52

Football Season in the Military 58

Military Racquetball & Football 61

Goodbye, Again 67

Part Three: U.S. Air Force Civil Service

Back to the World 76

The Sandbox Hotel 78

An Airman's Dream: Skating and Dianna 83

Homestead AFB 87

Part Four: Performing on the Main Stage

Career Moves 92

Alaska, Korea & Colin Powell 96

Part Five: Expanding the Military Family

Munchie Bear Arrives 106

Part Six: Seeing the World through an Airman's Eyes

Flying in the "Sand Box" 112

Two Weeks on the African Continent 115

The Philippines 118

Desert Storm: 1st Alert Launch 120

Sally 123

Volon Spouse Flights 124

Flying Dignitaries to Niagara Falls 125

Leaving Air Force One 131

Presidential Pushups 134

A Presidential Stop in Buffalo 135

Wind Turbulence on AF-1 138

President's Florida Injury 140

The Longest Day 141

President Clinton's Africa Trip 142

President Bush's Top-Secret Trip to Iraq 143

President Reagan's Funeral Flight 148

U.S. Presidential Campaigns 150

Clinton Reelection Campaign 153

2000 Gore Election Campaign 154

Chewing the Rag with the President 157

Putting My Faith to Work 159

JFK Career Days 161

Part Seven: Closing Doors & Starting a New Chapter

Tuskegee Airmen 164

Part Eight: Racquetball in My Veins

Racquetball 166

Oh, the People You Meet 182

Daddy's Almost Home 196

Part Nine: September 11, 2001

September 11, 2001 206

My Final Flight on the Big Plane 209

My Life After Retirement 220

Part Ten: Back to Where it All Began

Hello Again, Niagara Falls 234

Part Eleven: Memories

Family, Friends & Colleagues Share Memories......................238

Photographic Memories...276

Index...287

Foreword

There is an unsung power flowing through the rich history of Niagara Falls, New York. Quiet as it's kept, beyond the deafening rush of more than six million feet of cascading waters and a reputation as a honeymooner paradise, Niagara Falls has been both the birthplace and the destination for generations of Americans escaping injustice. These include early European immigrants, American slaves and some of the more than six million southern African Americans who moved north during the 20th century Great Migration. Jeffrey Elder's family was among them and he largely credits the city's unrelenting commitment to racial and social justice for propelling his unlikely journey of achievement and success.

I first met Jeffrey while traveling with President Bill Clinton on Air Force One. Jeffrey was one of the few African American military attendants on the plane. As the nation's first Black presidential speechwriter, I felt an immediate, if unspoken, bond between us. I instinctively understood that beneath his well-pressed uniform and professional demeanor, Jeffrey and I wore similar backgrounds.

It's a funny thing about the racial divide in America. Whether it is rooted in the inner-city projects of Baltimore, where I was born or the pristine lakes of Jeffrey Elder's Niagara Falls, it casts a similar aura around its survivors. The common ground we both shared at 30,000 feet was the desire to blaze new trails through the vehicle of service.

Jeffrey Elders' story is one of overcoming tremendous odds to give back to a nation and a city that he loves. He is fully aware of the legacy of discrimination that has hampered the progress of African Americans – from the Fugitive Slave Act of 1850 which accelerated the Underground Railroad's many stops in Niagara Falls to the toxic tragedy of Love Canal which inspired many African Americans to become part of our nation's nascent movement for environmental justice. But rather than give in to bitterness and defeat, Jeffrey Elder has chosen the path of service, faith and reconciliation. He has traveled the world and come back to where it all began to raise his family, to run for mayor, to be a servant leader.

W.E.B Dubois, who, in 1905, launched the Niagara Movement for civil rights in Niagara Falls, said "I believe that all men, black, brown, and white, are brothers." Jeffrey Elders' life of service is a testament to that truth. As America still struggles to overcome its past, his is a story that needs to be told.

J. Terry Edmonds

Former chief speechwriter for President William Jefferson Clinton

Introduction

Niagara Falls, the Honeymoon Capital of the World, has long been an exciting and romantic getaway for visitors and tourists from around the world. But, for mine and many other families in the city, it was a saving grace.

My parents began their migration to the strange, new place some 60 years ago, leaving behind a life of harsh and impoverished farming and sharecropping. The manufacturing companies changed the lives of so many people, for the better.

While we grew up knowing there was something special about our hometown that drew visitors from around the world, it was later in life that I actually took the time to research the story behind the city. It was then, that I learned the first recorded honeymoon trip to Niagara Falls was 1802 when Theodosia Burr, daughter of then U.S. Vice President Aaron Burr, visited the Falls with her husband, Joseph Alston. Reportedly, Napoleon Bonaparte's younger brother Jerome also visited Niagara with his bride in the early 1800s'.

Those high-profile visits were the start of a trend, and with the addition of railway lines and the opening of the Erie Canal, which made Niagara much more accessible to visitors, a growing number of couples began visiting Niagara Falls for their honeymoon. In the early 1900's the phrase "Honeymoon Capital of the World" was already being used in advertisements and brochures designed to encourage more visitors to Niagara.

With attractions such as the Maid of the Mist tour, based on the mythical young maiden who was captured by the God of Thunder and lived below the sea, the exciting helicopter rides over the falls, the Sky Wheel observation Ferris wheel, world-class shows and ample opportunities for memorable romantic walks and dinners. There is little wonder Niagara Falls remains a top destination for newlyweds from across the globe.

For people like me, who were lucky enough to call Niagara Falls home, it was easy to forget that every year people from all around the globe chose to dedicate their vacation time and money to visit Niagara.

Part One

The Love Canal

The Elder Family of Niagara Falls

I was born Saturday, February 10, 1962 at 10:28 a.m. I came here weighing 6 lbs. 7 oz. to Lula B. Elder, a single mother who already had two daughters. My father was not so much in the picture at this point but that would change over the years. My mother delivered me at the Niagara Falls Memorial Medical Center in Niagara Falls, NY. It was a cold, snowy morning which was usual for February in Western New York. This was the beginning of my Love Affair with this great City.

The first 18 years of my life I lived in the LaSalle area of Niagara Falls. It was a wonderful place to call home. During the time of my birth, my mother and two sisters lived on Allen Street, but shortly after we moved to Griffin Manor on 96th Street. I was too young to remember the address, but I do still have some memories of living there.

During the time of World War II, many people came to the city to work in the electro-chemical industries to support the war effort. One of the other premier companies was Bell Aerospace, a leader in aircraft and other aviation efforts.

The Elder family made up a large part of the Griffin Manor community. Most of us lived within blocks of each other. My Grandmother Lula Mae Elder, who her children called "Madea," lived at 1018, 95th Street. This was great for my mother and her siblings. They had a built-in babysitter.

When they went off to work, my grandmother took responsibility for watching over us. My cousins and I got to spend a lot of time together, and a lot of time with Granny, as we all called her.

Granny was born in Dozier, Alabama in 1906, to Lizzie Viola Mathews and Hilliard Mathews. She was the second born of eleven children. Following in her parents' footsteps, she would have ten children of her own. I often think back to how life must have been for her growing up in that time period and some of the things she saw and experienced. I can only guess they were not very good, given the fact that she moved all the way to Niagara Falls, NY in the late 1950's.

Granny was one of my favorite people in this world and I could never seem to get enough of being with her. She was very loving, but at the same time, tough. She was also the best cook that I have ever known. Everybody in the neighborhood would agree. Sundays were always a treat. Granny would cook and invite all family members that could make it over. It now amazed me that she was able to do this. You see, Granny was on a fixed income but there always seemed to be plenty to eat for everybody.

When it came to baking, Granny was second to none. It seemed that she always had some fresh cakes or pies in the pantry. I still can't help but smile remembering how, when Granny watched over us, she would often punish our transgressions by sending us to the pantry for time out.

What she never seemed to realize was that sending us to the pantry was not punishment for us—it was a perfect opportunity for us to sneak some of her baked goods she stored in the pantry, including her tea cakes, Lane Cakes and Sweet Potato Pie. Unfortunately, there was never any fried chicken there, because

Granny made the best fried chicken that I have ever tasted. I still regret that she somehow took the recipe with her when she passed away.

I would describe my grandmother as a Superhero, and a strong Black woman. She never had a driver's license but always found a way to get anywhere she wanted to go. She was also a very spiritual woman who loved the Lord and passed that faith and spirituality on to her family. She was certainly my hero, and I love her and will always miss her.

Griffon Manor

Griffon Manor was built in 1942, between 93rd and 96th streets on the west and east of Read Avenue, and at Bergholz Creek and Frontier Avenue on the north and south sides. The housing complexes were mainly constructed for families of the men and women who worked for Bell Aerospace.

After the war, Griffon Manor became a public housing project. The original 1942 buildings were replaced during the urban renewal projects of the 1970's. These later buildings were demolished during the remediation of The Love Canal in the 1980's.

Sometime around 1965 my family moved to another part of Griffon Manor. The address was 1007 Grant Drive, which was just 100 yards from 93rd Street School, the school I attended from Kindergarten to 6th grade. Unfortunately, 93rd Street School was demolished because it was located in the middle of the jurisdiction that was called "The Love Canal."

I have many memories of living at 1007 Grant Drive, but the most permanent memory is how spooky the area was. Even at a young age I felt uncomfortable there, as if there were other spirits there, especially when I was alone.

Surprisingly, we never actually talked about these feeling, but later I learned that one of my sisters had the same feeling about the area.

Our home, in the beginning of our move there, was heated by coal. We had coal bins in front of the house, and we would have to shovel coal into the furnace to warm the house. One of my favorite pastimes was playing in the coal bins. As you can imagine, that was not fun for my mother who had to clean my clothes.

—

Mom had a 1967 Galaxy 500 convertible. I absolutely loved that car, but I have no idea why my mom even bought it since she was very particular about her hair. My mother had beautiful hair, and never wanted to get it messed up. She also hated heat and avoided the sun like the plague. I guess she loved her children quite a bit, because every now and then we would get a special treat when she let down the top and took us for a ride around the Falls just for the fun of it. This was another childhood experience that would direct my future. To this day, I'm in love with convertibles.

When I was in Kindergarten, all the little boys thought my teacher was just the bomb – me, included. Ms. Baker was her name, and I had a serious crush on her as did all the other little boys in my class. But there was a little girl in my class that I also thought was kind of neat. Her name was Valerie. One day I got really bold and gave Valerie a kiss.

She went home and told her dad and the next day when she came in, she told me that her dad said that if I kissed her again to sock me right in the nose. Well I was done with kissing Valerie. In spite of her ending our love affair, we remained friends all through High School. My mother once said she knew I was going to be a handful when one day she saw me walking home from 93rd Street Elementary School and a little girl was carrying my books.

Not having a brother, my cousin Tommie and I were as close as brothers could be. We would do most everything together. We were like two peas in a pod, you would rarely see one of us without the other. Whenever anyone took family photos, Tommie and I would always find a way to sneak in the photo. We often got into trouble together especially when playing cards or Pokeno for pennies.

Tommie and I also fought a lot. When one would win all the money the other would try to wrestle it back. On one occasion,

Tommie won all my money and was trying to leave to go home. There was no way I was letting him leave with all my pennies. We started wrestling and got so wild that we broke the leg on the kitchen table. At that point, I don't think the money mattered, because we forgot about the fight and instantly started working together to get the table to stand up with a broken leg before my mother got home.

We finally managed to get it to stay up, and when Mom came home, we were sitting quiet like two little church mice. When she set her purse on the table, it immediately fell over. Tommie and I pretended surprise, asking mom what happened. My mom looked at us and knew we were up to no good. She forced us to confess. We would all later laugh about it, but at the time no one laughed. Wrestling was huge, back then. We watched it faithfully on television, and no one could convince us that any part of wrestling was fake. We took it so seriously that we made a nearly full-size wrestling ring in the field behind my cousin's house. Every young kid in the neighborhood seemed to have showed up. They would all use a famous wrestler's name, like Bobo Brazil, Texas Calhoun and Ernie the Cat Ladd. Of course, I was "The Mighty Igor." Even a few of the girls in our community participated and used wrestlers' names as well. We made championship belts out of cardboard and aluminum foil. We had a great time with our ring until the Housing Authority came and tore it down. Not even that stopped us from loving wrestling. We just had to act it out without using a ring.

—

My mother worked a second job as a waitress for a while. She would bring home impressive tips and deposit them into a huge bottle that had a one-way slot in it. One day, I figured out a way to use a butter knife to force coins to fall through the bottle top. With my stolen coins, I would go to the store right across the street and buy all kinds of goodies. I must have been going on a daily basis because over time, my sisters became suspicious. One day, my sister asked, "How is it that you always seem to have money in your pockets?"

I told them I was getting the money from a kid at school named Francis Hanson. This went on for a while till one day my sisters cornered Francis and asked him why he keeps giving me money. Of course, Francis had no idea what they were talking about and totally denied everything. My little scheme came to an end, and I started looking for a legitimate way to keep coins in my pocket.

My cousin Tommie and I teamed up and started our own little business shoveling sidewalks in the winter and mowing lawns in the summer. We would also run errands for neighbors, including going to the store and picking up things they needed. We would never get rich, but it was an honest way to earn enough money to purchase the things we wanted. Both Tommie's and my sisters, however, would always find ways to help us spend our money. They would plan small parties and Tommie and I would have to supply all the goodies.

They built a new Griffon Manor in the early 1970's. My family moved to 524 95th Street which was in Court 4.

There were 12 Courts in all with a total of 250 housing units and there were Elder family members in six of the twelve. It was at this new home that I finally got my own room for the first time. We lived in a town house with three bedrooms, a basement, but only one bathroom. Imagine growing up in a house with three females, and you are the only male and the youngest and there is only one bathroom. My bathroom time was little to none. Yet, I still had my own room, with bunk beds for my cousin Tommie who was always over, when I wasn't at his home.

The Love Canal

The Love Canal was originally meant to be a dream community as envisioned by William T. Love, an ambitious entrepreneur. In the 1890's, Love wanted to create a "Model City." He was going to dig a canal in Western New York State from the Niagara River, around Niagara Falls, and into Lake Ontario. Love was going to use the waterflow through this canal to generate electricity for this new community in which he mapped out parks and community centers, roads and neighborhoods.

The vision was a great one, but congress passed a law in May 1913 prohibiting the diversion of water out of the Niagara River to help preserve one of the Wonders of the World—the famous falls. Love then built a few houses and ran out of money and abandoned his project.

In the 1920's the City of Niagara Falls began using the canal as a dump site for garbage and in 1942 the Hooker Electric Company was given permission to use the canal as a dump site for their chemical waste. The waste was in 55-gallon drums and had about 21,000 tons of very toxic chemicals that was buried there. In 1953 Hooker Electric sold this land area for $1 to the City of Niagara Falls. 99th Street School and several neighborhoods to include a 54-unit senior citizen development and the 250-unit housing project called Griffon Manor were built on and around The Love Canal.

Since that time, the neighborhood was known as a 70-acre landfill which became the cause of a massive environmental pollution disaster harming the health of hundreds of residents, culminating in an extensive Superfund cleanup operation.

It turns out that every home we lived in, in Griffon Manor, was located within The Love Canal, and two schools were situated within that dangerous zone as well.

—

I attended, 93rd Street from kindergarten through sixth grade; LaSalle Junior High School, and LaSalle Senior High. Only LaSalle Junior High is still standing today, and it was renamed LaSalle Preparatory School. This happened because 93rd Street was located within The Love Canal zone. Another school, 99th Street School was also within this zone, and had to be demolished. My older sisters and many other family members attended 99th Street School. I enjoyed attending the junior high school during my ninth grade, as opposed to being a freshman in the High School. This, however, presented another problem. I wanted to play football and practices were held at LaSalle Sr. High. So that meant that every day after school, I would have to ride my bicycle all the way over to LaSalle Sr. High to attend practice. It was a lot, but I was getting to play football and the extra riding helped in my conditioning.

As a ninth grader we were the big guys of the school and treated the underclassman as underlings. We had a Class Day, and even had a Class Song. Our Class Song was *Hotel California* by The Eagles. We all liked the part of the song that said, "You can check out any time you want, but you can never leave." As much as I enjoyed my time there, I eventually did check out for my final school years at LaSalle Sr. High School.

I arrived at LaSalle Sr. High as a sophomore. I was already friends with some of the upperclassmen. While I was in ninth grade, I had made friends with some of the football players, which meant they saw me as something of a junior veteran. I had had my hazing as a freshman player and paid my dues, so I knew what was in store for the younger guys. We all accepted it as a rite of passage.

Born to Travel

My first road trip was in 1967 when my Uncle James, who we all called "Biscuit," took me and my mother to Dozier, Alabama, where they were born. I was fortunate to have Uncles that lived out of state or often traveled out of state. I was five years old, and at that point in my life, my father was not a permanent fixture in my life. All of my uncles, though, were the next best thing to having a constant father in my life.

The trip to Alabama was an eye-opening experience for a young boy who knew only about the city of Niagara Falls, and nothing about the rural south. I quickly learned, however, how different it was from what I was used to.

The drive from Niagara Falls to Dozier, Alabama was long, to say the least—1,076 miles. While, today, it takes about 18 hours to drive, back in 1967, before endless freeways, the drive was more like 22-24 hours. Not only was it a long ride, but our car was packed with six adults and children.

Uncle Biscuit and mom were the designated drivers and did all the driving. It was as if they were in competition to see who could drive the fastest. I sat up front, in the middle, and witnessed each of them exceed 100 miles per hour. For a five-year old, I didn't know to be scared. The faster the cooler. Unfortunately, it also set a precedent for my future driving habits—driving and speeding are one and the same.

Dozier was the country personified, "straight up in the woods." Some places were so far back into the woods that when you drove around corners, you had to blow your horn to alert oncoming drivers that you were coming through. When we arrived at my great uncle's house, my grandmother's brother, it was pitch black.

No street lights. No yard lights. I immediately announced that I had to use the bathroom. My Aunt grabbed a flashlight, took my hand, and proceeded out the door. Confused, I wondered did she understand that I had to use the bathroom. She did. She was taking me to the bathroom—an outhouse that was built in the back of the house. "Go ahead baby," she said. "Use the bathroom."

I looked into the small construction, then back at my Aunt. I was in shock, and immediately announced that I no longer had to use the bathroom. In my five years, I had never heard of an outhouse before. Needless to say, my first trip to Alabama was an eye-opening experience for this five- year-old.

—

I began visiting my uncle "Son," who was in the Air Force, in 1973. Every three years I would travel to his home and spend the summer with him and his family. This was when I realized the differences in spending time in a two-parent home. While I knew my father my father, he was not yet a regular presence in my home or in my life. He lived just miles from us, on the other side of town, but we very seldom spent any time together. Again, my uncles filled that void.

In the summer of 1973, my uncle had visited the family in Niagara Falls, and asked my mother if I could go back with him for the rest of the summer. I was very excited about this trip. We drove 10 hours, before arriving at Hampton, Virginia. It was a much shorter trip than the one we took to Dozier, Alabama, and I no longer had to worry about outhouses. I visited my uncle at Langley Air Force Base.

My uncle lived in the Base Housing unit called Bayview Towers, a high rise located right on the waterfront. We were able to go to the pier and fish almost at any time. This is where I was introduced to a fish called croaker. The name croaker is descriptive of the noise the fish makes by vibrating strong muscles against its swim bladder, and this acts as a resonating chamber much like a ball. Once I caught one, I was so fascinated looking and listening to it that I totally forgot about fishing and almost lost my pole when another one took my bait.

My summer was filled with lots of fun, including our road trip to Christiansburg, VA., where my aunt's parents lived. Though Christiansburg was situated all the way on the other side of Virginia, it was a beautiful ride all the way there. The town is nestled in the Blue Ridge Mountains and has the most amazing mountain views anywhere in the world.

I have never been attracted to the outdoors, but for whatever reason, a camping trip we took on my Uncle Otis's land was fun and memorable. My Aunt's family instantly treated me as I was part of their immediate family. I loved everything about this trip— from waking up early, to the smell of simmering apples Ms. Alverta cooked each morning, to the wonderful dinners with us all sitting around the table eating and talking.

Christiansburg was also my first time seeing "Lightening Bugs." I was fascinated by these flying lights. My cousin Tony and I would run around catching them all night until we were told to go to bed. My aunt's father had built the house we stayed in that summer. It had started out a lot smaller than what we experienced. He had continuously added to his home, over the years. Even as a child I was impressed with the sturdy foundation. I imagined he had to put a lot of time, money, hard work and pride into building his home, and it showed.

Much too fast, it was time for us to travel back to Hampton. The summer was coming to an end. Mom would be driving down to pick me up in just two weeks. What had, up to then, been a fun vacation turned into complete chaos during my last week in Hampton. My mother drove down with my two sisters to pick me up. But, unbeknownst to us, one of my other aunts drove down separately – all the way from Niagara Falls, to Hampton, Virginia in a Torino, filled with seven adults. This group immediately made it known that their express purpose for coming to Hampton was to "party." While it was pretty insane, they ended up having a great time, even though my uncle lived in a three-bedroom apartment. Somehow, everybody settled in and made the best of it.

—

In 1976 I spent the summer with my Uncle Son and his family at McGuire, AFB near Trenton, NJ. A young man by the name of Antonio lived just across from my uncle, and we immediately became friends. Antonio, his brother, my younger cousin and I spent the entire summer hanging out and getting into mischief. My uncle had a Ford Truck with a Camper on the back. The four of us boys would spend many a night in the camper talking about who we were going to date and what we were going to be when we grew up.

I had joined the Civil Air Patrol (CAP), an auxiliary of the US Air Force in high school, and knew I wanted to join the Air Force like my uncle. I was really proud to be part of CAP. It was a Total Force partner that took part in searches for missing persons, provided comfort to families in times of disaster, and worked to keep the communities safe. I would proudly talk about my role in CAP during those long nights with my cousin and Antonio. Of course, there was some talk about a girl named Misty who Antonio knew, but showed no real interest.

That summer, I met a neighborhood bully named Walt who it seemed everyone was deathly afraid of. When I met him, he tried to intimidate me, but it didn't work. Instead, I laughingly called him "Jelly Belly," and walked away... actually, I ran away, with Walt in swift pursuit. Luckily, I managed to keep my distance from him for the rest of the summer, and that was because of the girl named Misty.

I met Misty and was immediately smitten. I'd had crushes before, but this was the first time I really fell for a girl. To my luck, my cousin Alicia and Misty were friends. And my second luck was that Misty lived just a few doors down. We were both kids, so nothing serious happened, but for me just holding Misty's hand was "something." Of course, my cousins, all younger, had no idea what was going on. They had no idea I had been bitten by the love bug.

—

Hurricane Bell came to the East Coast that summer of 1976. I had never experienced a hurricane, before, and being young and ignorant about the tragedies left behind by hurricanes, I initially viewed this as another fun experience. I began to realize how serious the hurricane was when all the aircraft at the Base left for safer areas, and all the base residents still there, were directed to bunker down. We woke up the next day to unbelievable destruction. everything was strewn all over the place. That was when I learned about the dangers of hurricanes.

It was a great summer. We did a lot more this time. I saw my first professional baseball game in Philadelphia. The Philadelphia Phillies against the Pittsburgh Pirates. How can I forget that game, with legends like Willie Stargell, Mike Schmidt and Dave Parker who hit an in the park home run? We also visited the Great Adventure amusement park, and made another trip to Christiansburg, VA.

Finally, my summer came to an end. In late August, my mom drove to New Jersey and picked me up. When I arrived back in Niagara

Fall, for the first time I noticed the difference in the weather in Niagara and how quickly our summers came to an end. That summer was also the last time I saw Misty, the girl of my dreams—for one summer. We wrote each other a few times, but the love bug slowly faded over the next months.

—

In 1978, my mother and two of her sisters caught a Grey Hound bus, from Niagara Falls, to Vacaville, California. The trip was a four-day bus ride. While they enjoyed their trip, when it was time to return home some of them decided a plane ride would be just as much fun. The next year my mother thought it would be a great adventure for me to take the four-day bus ride from Niagara Falls to Vacaville.

I was 17 years old, and beyond excited to be traveling coast to coast all alone. This was the farthest that I had ever traveled. Even then, I was beginning to love traveling, and during this trip I was able to see a lot of the Country. By the time I reached Vacaville, I was in need of a long hot shower and some real food. My wonderful aunt was right there to take care of me. I always loved going to visit them because they treated me as one of their own.

Many of our days were spent, running through the house playing; trying to ensure that we didn't break anything. But, you know we broke a few things. This being my first time to California, I knew absolutely nothing about Black Widow Spiders other than "I was afraid of them". My cousin Tony, being a jokester saw an opportunity to mess with me. As we were playing running inside and out, then, Tony said "Jeffrey, there is a Black Widow on your back". At first, I froze in my tracks. I then frantically ripped off my shirt. However, when I looked up, both of my cousins were laughing hysterically. Ok, they got me! I guess it was just payback for my many pranks.

My uncle was Air Crewmember for the Air Force and had to travel during my time at his home. I still greatly enjoyed my time with my aunt and cousins. On my uncle's return, he would take us all out to places like San Francisco, where we hung out at the Fisherman's Wharf, and even to an Oakland A's baseball game.

My uncle knew that I was a pretty good roller-skater, so he and my aunt took me to the Fairfield Roller Rink. It was a great opportunity for me to show off my New York style of Boogie Skating. I met a lot of new friends there and was able to teach my moves to some of them.

Before I knew it, the summer was coming to a close. It was time for me to start my long trek back to Niagara Falls—four days on the Greyhound again.

Somehow, I wasn't as excited about the return trip, but it wasn't bad, after all. I was still excited about seeing so much of the country. I barely slept, thinking I might miss something.

There is no question that my summers away from Niagara Falls with my uncles who were like fathers to me, made a world of difference in who I became. I am so grateful for their love, their patience and all that they shared with me during my young years.

I am especially grateful that those summers allowed me and my cousin Tony to become extremely close. And, while Tony is no longer with us, I have such wonderful memories of our times together. My aunt felt his loss probably more than any of us. I made a special effort to comfort her during that time, and to let her know that though she had lost one son, I was there and would always be that other son for her. While we're miles apart, I believe our shared love for Tony will always keep us near.

Finding my Father

I didn't have to go far to find my father. Willie George Johnson was not more than a few miles from me the whole time, yet, for most of my childhood, Willie Johnson was not a major part of my life. In fact, I'd say he missed out on the most impressionable years of my young life.

The story about my Mom and Dad, I learned later, was that they were scheduled to get married before my birth, but for some, yet unexplained reason, the wedding was cancelled at the last minute. That left my mother a single parent and left me a fatherless child.

So, I came into this world with the last name of Elder and not Johnson. While I fully embrace my last name of Elder, I also know that the blood that runs through my veins includes my father's blood—the Johnsons.

What fatherless child would not be jubilant to learn that they are not actually fatherless? That you have a father, and he actually lives just across town from you and your mother? I remember that day like it was yesterday. My mother and father sat me down and together told me Willie George Johnson was actually my father. I was elated, I finally knew who my dad was. What I didn't know then, but felt without understanding, is that a young boy needs to know and have a relationship with his father. It is a special and much needed passage of life, especially in the African American community.

Unfortunately, mine and my father's relationship didn't blossom from that first meeting. We didn't automatically begin doing things together or hanging out after that. The reason, I rationalized, was that my father was married and had a family. So, I spent the first fifteen years of my life knowing that I had a father, and other siblings and family members across town but not really interacting with them.

On occasion I would call my father to see if he would come over for a visit. He didn't. Eventually, when I called and his family knew it was me, they would tell me he wasn't home. I began to call and disguise my voice to sound like an adult or use his brother-in-law Frank's name. That would always get him on the phone. When he realized it was me, he never got angry. He would tell me what I wanted to hear... that we would get together soon. I fell for it every time.

On one occasion when I called my father's home, my stepmother answered the phone. When I asked for my father she asked, "Where is your mother? Put her on the phone." When my mother answered the phone, the two of them had a rather heated conversation. My stepmother asked Mom why I was continuously calling her house. My mother told her it was because I wanted to speak to my father, and I had a right to call him. I didn't hang around to listen to the rest of the conversation as I realized both of them were getting upset.

All I ever wanted was to have a real relationship with my father. Because of that need, I treasured even more my close relationships with my uncles. It was my uncles who taught me the values and lessons I'd need as a man. They were the ones who spent the time nourishing my need to be around a father figure. To all of them I say thank you for helping me to become the man that I am today.

I was the youngest child in my mother's home, but I had younger sisters I didn't grow up with. Looking back, I wish I could have spent time with my younger sisters and watch them grow into the beautiful women they are. Thankfully, we have all embraced the fact that we are siblings based on the simple fact of who are parents are. While we may not agree with all our parents did in the past, we've learned to accept them, and to move on to enjoy the years we have together.

As a young man, I would sometimes listen to the Harry Chapin song *The Cat's in the Cradle*. I remember how sad it always made me. But, most importantly the words forced me to make a commitment to myself that I would never be the kind of absent father in that song, and would do everything in my power to be there for my children. The song did something else: it made me realize that, though it was imperfect, my relationship with my father was priceless and I would do anything I could to mend that relationship.

—

Mine and my father's relationship did improve during my teenage years. By the time I graduated from high school it would be on even keel and would continue that way. As I'd dreamed of doing all my life; after graduation, I went into the military. As I prepared to leave for my first assignment in Germany, I realized that I had never told my father that I loved him. I began to realize I was going all the way to the other side of the world, a long way from home with no guarantee I'd ever see him again. That was the first time I told my father I loved him, but not the last. It quickly became a standard goodbye every time we talked on the phone or visited.

In January 2013, my father had a massive heart attack. His doctors had to perform a quintuple bypass which was successful. Though his operation was a success, he was forced to slow down. All in all, there is no mistaking it; I am my father's son. We are so alike in many ways both good and bad. I love you Pops. It is close calls like this one that reminds us of our regrets, like the one I still have that when I retired from the Air Force and family and friends came, I failed to acknowledge my father. Though I've apologized for the oversight, this is probably as good a time as ever to say it again: Pops, I apologize and you know I love you.

The Carousel Skate Center

The Carousel Skate Center was my home away from home. I finally found something that I could excel in. Growing up in Niagara Falls, there was enough trouble to get into, but the Carousel was my refuge and definitely kept me out of trouble, for the most part.

Disco was in, and I loved Disco music. I could dance pretty good so I would try to skate the same way I danced. In the beginning, I didn't have my own skates so I would rent them at the rink. I remember always trying different moves and busting my butt a lot. My friends would say they didn't fall all night and I would reply, I fell a lot, but I learned a different move.

A friend named Scott gave me my first pair of skates. Yes, hand-me-downs, but the first time I put them on I was able to do all those moves better and a lot easier. I immediately started to fall less, and even started wearing nicer clothes so I would look good as I skate-danced. At the rink, we didn't just roller-skate, we Boogie Skated! You just had to be there to believe it.

The rink became the place I spent most all of my spare time. On Sundays there were three sessions. 10 a.m. to noon was for youngsters and beginners. 1-4 p.m. was for families skating together, and 7-10 p.m. was for everyone. Sundays were Soul Night. On Soul Night, if you couldn't skate, you shouldn't be on the floor. On these nights, the rink was always packed, and skaters went hard and fast. When one person fell, it was like a domino effect—everybody fell. Monday and Thursday nights were for private parties.

Tuesdays were adult night with organ music—a real organ. What I remember best about Tuesday nights was Pop Dorato, who most people called Pop D. Pop D was my best friend's father who I also called Dad. He also happened to be the coolest person in the rink. As Pop D would skate by, all the ladies would turn their heads and sigh, but his wife Nancy was always right by his side with that little smile that said, "Hey ladies, you can look but he is all mine." My friends and I who had snuck in, would sit watching and laughing. Pop D. had all the moves down. I even got a few from him. I just wasn't as cool as him... yet.

Wednesday nights were Cheapskate Night. It only cost $1.50 to get in on Wednesdays, and back then I was all about Cheapskate Night. Friday night included two sessions: 7-10 regular skating, and 11-2, late skating. You had to be 18 years old for late skating. That gave me an excuse to be out late. Saturday had two sessions: from 1-4 p.m. and 7:30-11:30 p.m., our time to shine. Young people from all the schools in the area would come out to the Saturday night 7:30 sessions.

Ed Murray was the rink manager. One day he saw me standing, watching skaters go by and asked me if I liked coming there. I told him, yes. He then told me something that has stayed with me, that what you have to do is find something that you like doing and learn to do it so well that you will get paid for it. I told him that made sense to me. Most surprising, he then asked if I'd like to work for him at the rink. Not believing I was hearing what he said correctly, I asked, "You mean, you want to pay me for being here?" My mother didn't raise no fool... I gladly accepted.

Mr. Ed Murray's words stick with me to this day and have been a guiding force in my career decisions. He was an excellent boss who would never ask an employee to do anything he would not do first. I learned a great deal from his style of leadership. Things that I practice even to this day.

Danny O. had the coolest pair of skates I'd seen. They were called

Micro-Star 2500; all precision roller-skates. I absolutely loved them. When Danny asked me one day if I wanted to buy them, I couldn't get the money out of my pocket fast enough. I knew the quality of roller-skates, and the Micro-Star 2500 was top notch, extremely heavy compared to the ordinary skate plate. They fit perfectly with the way I skated, allowing me to do maneuvers that others couldn't manage. Once I bought Danny O's skates, it was game on for Boogie Skating. I loved them so much, I never got rid of them, though I worked them pretty hard, and they ended up in need of repair.

The Carousel had its own style. We recognized when skaters from other places came in. There was an outstanding group of skaters from Canada that came every week, and always competed against us in the "Boogie Skate" competition. The DJ would make a special announcement: "Boogie Skaters only, on the floor. If you are not an advanced Boogie Skater, please leave the floor."

The entire Canada group was outstanding, but one of them stood out among the rest. His name was Mike, and he was an amazing Boogie Skater. Winning the Boogie Skate Competition was always the highlight of the night; but when Mike was there competing, it was really tough.

Though we were serious competitors, I have to admit I learned some moves from him.

Mike stopped coming after a while. We later learned that he had gotten in some trouble and could not come across the border. I started missing those competitions with Mike. The competition got so strong, however, that the rink formed the Carousel Boogie Team. Everybody wanted to be a member of the Boogie Team and get to wear the shirt.

When we went to other rinks, either for competitions or just to skate, we wore our shirts and usually took over the place. Once I started working at the Carousel Rink, I no longer could participate in the Boogie Skate Competition, there. I was still able to travel to other rinks and compete. And I did so, regularly.

My Carousel Boogie Team shirt read "King Jammer." I took great pride in leading the team and being an example when we traveled to other rinks to skate. Usually, we didn't just skate when we went to other rinks; we took over, in a good way.

I had become a very good skater. In my first Boogie Skate competition, I was sure I was going to win, but came in second place. I couldn't believe it. Turns out, the winner was a female—Joanne—a few years older. Joanne could skate like nothing I'd ever seen. We eventually teamed up, and as a team we became unbeatable. We competed at the Cocoa Cola Roller Disco Championship and collected the first-place trophy at the Carousel in West Seneca, NY. We also became best of friends, and she would later become Aunt Joanne to my daughters. True friendship is hard to find, but when you do find it, it is priceless. Thank you, Joanne, for being that true friend.

The Carousel Skating Center gave me so many great memories—including my first real kiss with Shannon, behind the Carousel. I was a huge flirt, but I was mostly all talk. Well, I talked myself into an unexpected kiss by a girl I thought wasn't willing. To my great surprise, she was more than willing, grabbing me by the hand and pulling me behind the rink where she proceeded to put her tongue into my mouth. I was thinking to myself: *How did I not know about this*? It felt great! Shannon gave me my first real kiss, but strangely, we never dated. I really was mostly all talk. I wanted to hold on to my innocence as long as I could. And I did.

One of the Carousel's greatest contributions to the Niagara Falls community was that it was a cultural melting pot.

People from all different walks of life, and all ethnicities came together there to try and learn this thing we called "Boogie Skating." It was also good for youth; a refuge for young people who may have ended up on the streets where they could easily get into trouble. Not to say there was no trouble to get into at the rink, but this was a controlled environment and the core skaters and many of the rink parents, like mom and pop Dorato, Mr. & Mrs. Emmons and of course Mrs. Murphy to name a few, would not let things get out of control most of the time. Imagine, we could actually settle our differences by out-skating our opponent.

—

My first job at the rink was as a skate room attendant. I would hand out skates and work on other skates to keep them rolling. Next, I became a floor guard, which was a lot more difficult. I had to always skate backwards to help those who fell and keep fast skaters under control. When the Boogie Skate Competition came up, the floor guards would choose who would be in the finals and then the crowd would choose the winner. My last job at the Carousel was as Disc Jockey (DJ). That was extremely hard. I had to play all the good music and watch everybody else skate to it. It got to the point that I would bring my skates into the DJ booth, put on a good song and go out and skate to it. The boss was not crazy about that, but would allow it on certain occasions.

I admit I'm not proud of all the things I did at the rink, but they happened and they're part of my story, so I will share them with you.

—

The Carousel had a New Year's Eve celebration, and I was the DJ that night. At that time, I wore platform shoes. Yes, platforms. They happened to be in style, then. Because they were very tight, I wore nylon socks with them; and, when I put on my skates, I would add white tube socks under my nylons. Of course, I would have to take off the tube socks to fit back into my platforms when it was time to leave.

On this particular evening, I drove my mom's car. My two best friends Paul and Dave Dorato were riding with me. All the Carousel employees were given Christmas Stockings for the holidays, and it so happened the stockings contained miniature bottles of alcohol—mine was 151 Rum. The later the night got, the more miniature bottles we drank. Too late, I realized I was intoxicated. Yes, innocent Jeffrey Elder was drunk. As I said, I owe a lot of my life lessons to the Carousel Rink. This was my first time experiencing being drunk, and to my even greater surprise—blacking out. The last thing I remembered was friends and I being at the rink. The next thing I knew, I was waking up in my bed at home.

When I woke up the next morning, I wondered what the heck happened and how did I get home. I realized I was still fully dressed but my white tube socks were extremely dirty on the bottom. At that point I began worrying that I might have walked home and left my mother's car at the rink. I called my partners in crime Paul and Dave who lived right behind me and asked what happened. They both started laughing and told me the story.

When it came time for them to put on my shoes, there was no way that those platform shoes were fitting on my feet over those tube socks. So, they just walked me out to my car in my socks. Next, they had to get me in the car. As they explained, this was a feat in itself. I was all over the place and not cooperating. Finally, they got me in, and Paul the older and more responsible one drove us home. They managed to get me in my front door and then they ran home fearing my mom would catch all of us. From all accounts, as soon as I went through that front door, I straightened up enough to go upstairs to my room, where I promptly fell out in my bed.

I was totally relieved to know that, first I didn't walk home; and second, I didn't drink and drive. Most of all, I was relieved that my mother didn't see me in that condition. As for 151 Rum, after that night I would cringe anytime I heard the name. Happily, that was my one and only experience of drinking. And by the way, I also gave up wearing platform shoes.

—

One of my fondest memories of the rink was my going away party. The owners and manager of the rink closed the doors on one of the busiest nights to throw me a going away party. It was by invitation only, so I got to choose who attended. I was very pleased when my mom got there. She had not been on roller-skates in over twenty years and we thought it would be great to have her go around the rink a few times.

What were we thinking? Paul, Dave and I put her skates on and entered the skate floor next to the DJ booth. About 40 minutes later, we made it to the nearest exit about 45 feet away. We were all exhausted and Instructed my mom to take off those skates and just watch! Of course, we laughed about it later but at the time it wasn't so funny.

At my going away party, I was presented with a wonderful cake with a roller-skate on it that said, "Good luck, Jeff." I was also given a doll that was hand made to look like me. It even had eggshell teeth and was wearing a pair of Carousel clip-on roller-skates. The best gift, by far, was the bright orange jacket baring the name, Carousel Skate CTR, NF, NY, along with my name on the front. I was overwhelmed. I had no idea the staff there would actually miss me this much. The feeling, however, was definitely mutual, and I didn't want the party to end.

That night as I stood in the DJ both for the last time, I looked over the rink and into the crystal ball hanging in the middle of the rink. I thought to myself: *Whenever I look at a crystal ball, I will think about this moment at the Carousel Skating Center.*

On the Cusp of Adulthood

It turned out I was quite an athlete. I never knew exactly whose genes those were, but they were there. In high school, I lettered in football, wrestling and track. I didn't really excel in any of them, but they were great learning experiences. The toughest of those was wrestling. Three, two-minute periods seemed like a week on the mats. My coach Mr. Philacetti told us that with wrestling you will be in the best physical condition in your life. Boy, was he right! During my senior year I only needed a few credits to graduate so my day at school ended at 11:30 a.m. I would then return later for after school activities.

One of those activities was the Key Club. Key Club is an international, student-led organization that provides its members with opportunities to provide service, build character and develop leadership. Key Club members around the world learn how to lead and stand for what's right through service and volunteerism. In partnership with the local Kiwanis club, our high school students were involved in a number of positive initiatives that served our school, and the community. I became the Vice President of our Key Club, and would often have lunch with the Kiwanis members, at the Alps Restaurant, across from LaSalle Senior High School.

The Key Clubs had a state convention every year in South Fallsburg, NY at the Pines Hotel and Resort in the Catskill Mountains. This was a fun weekend where our chaperones would drive us to and from the festivities. One of my most memorable activities there, was our final banquet that was held in the Persian Room. It was a fun evening, highlighted by a little mischief.

My last day as a student at LaSalle High School was bittersweet for me. Many of us just hung out signing year books and talking about what we were going to do with our lives. When I walked out the doors for the last time, a friend snapped a few pictures to be able to look back years later and remember that moment in time.

Many of my classmates wanted our class song to be *After the Love* by Earth, Wind and Fire. Unfortunately, a number of students disagreed and voted it down. We ended up with *Free Bird* by Lynyrd Skynyrd. I've always been the sentimental type and have to believe that if those students could make that choice again, they'd pick *After the Love*.

Our Prom night took place on Friday the 13th. My father loaned me his car that night—his 1973 Electra 225; also known as "Deuce and a Quarter." I really thought that night, I was looking as cool as my dad usually did in his car. Cynthia was my girlfriend, and my date for the night. Before leaving to pick her date, I posed for pictures with one of my best friends, Emery; my mom, granny, and Aunt Tommie. I left then, to pick up Cynthia, who looked outstanding that night.

Cynthia and I met Emery and Danny and their dates, for a three-car convoy heading to the Riverside Inn, in Lewiston for the prom. Emery, who had only had his license for three weeks, led the way. We were running late, so we decided to put the pedal to the medal. As Emery passed a vehicle, I saw the driver reach over and put on a hat. Not just any hat, but the Campaign Hat usually worn by State Troopers. By this time, I was on my brakes, and side by side with the Trooper. He directed all three cars to pull over. There we were, standing on Interstate 190 dressed to the max in fine cars and all getting tickets. The Trooper said we were going 75 MPH in a 55 MPH zone. We pleaded our case that we were late for the Prom, to no avail. We were now going to be even later.

We didn't let this ruin our evening, and took our time getting to the prom from there. I recall being a little salty at the prom during the occasion that the guys take off the ladies' garter. My date didn't have one, and I didn't know that I was supposed to provide her with it. I was still a little naïve when it came to the ladies.

Graduation day was June 22, 1980. LaSalle Senior High, along with all the other high schools in the city, had our commencement ceremony at the Niagara Falls Convention Center, which would later become Seneca Niagara Casino. During its heyday, the convention Center was constantly in demand. Every high school graduation, many local university sports events, plus for three years, the televised Miss USA Pageant, hosted by Bob Barker.

After graduation, my family had a graduation party for me, and a birthday party for Mom and me, as we shared that day in celebration. We all got to celebrate together one more time before my life would change considerably.

Part Two

On Becoming a Man

The Hair Cut

The Last Day of School

I signed up for the Delayed Enlistment Program to join the Air Force on January 9, 1980. Six months prior to my High School Graduation. My mother had to sign the consent because I was under the age of 18.

It seemed like those eight months flew by. I will never forget the morning of August 1, 1980. That was the day my mother drove me to the recruiters' station on Pine Avenue in Niagara Falls to leave for the Air Force. In all the excitement preparing for my departure I hadn't been prepared for the emotion of leaving my mother. I quickly realized what all this meant. I was moving away from my mother and family who had been my life all these years. We weren't just a family, we were a deeply involved family. For me there was excitement and anticipation of new beginnings, but also fear of being alone without family members that had always been there.

It was most likely because I was my mother's only son and her youngest child that made our relationship a very special one. I can recall our last embrace before we parted. I hadn't realized it before, but I knew this was going to be a very painful experience for my mom, watching me leave home. Not only was I leaving home, but I was going off to serve my country and she didn't know whether I'd ever return. As my mom drove off, I became even more emotional as I saw her sobbing uncontrollably as she drove off.

My recruiter, Richard Cadille, made me feel a lot better by telling me that everything would be fine, that these were always difficult moments for mothers and their sons. He also let me know that I was doing the right thing. I thought, cynically, that he would say that since my joining helped him make his quota for the month. We drove to Buffalo to the Military Enlisted Processing (MEPs) station where I took the official Oath to join the Air Force. From there, all new recruits were herded onto a bus to the airport and off to San Antonio, Texas.

Allow me to tell you about San Antonio, Texas in early August. August is the hottest month in Texas. When we landed and was herded to another bus to take us to the base, it was late and still hot. Our first encounter once we got off the bus at Lackland Air Force Base (AFB) was a Training Instructor (TI) yelling at us to get in formation.

I was previously in the Civil Air Patrol, so I knew what he was talking about. But most others had no clue. We were all tired and were all wondering: *What the heck did we get ourselves into*?

Well, the yelling didn't stop. Once we got in formation with our bags, the TI instructed us to pick up our bags. Then, put them down. Pick them up; now put them down. Were they confused? This went on for twenty minutes. If you weren't tired before, you were by the end of those 20 minutes.

Finally, we made it to our dormitory, our new home for the next six weeks and four days. I was assigned to Flight 153 which was part of the 3708 Basic Military Training Squadron (BMTS). Technical Sergeant (TSgt) West was our TI. His uniform was so sharp that we wondered how he even got in it.

It seemed as if we had only just fallen asleep when the yelling resumed: "Drop your bleeps and grab your socks. Get up!"

Still sleepy, I thought: *You have got to be kidding me.*

I had five minutes to be downstairs in formation, after brushing my teeth and combing my hair. I had a very nice sized afro that I was quite proud of, when I went into Basic Training. A couple of days later, they had taken care of that. It was gone. We had to stand in formation in front of the barber shop. One by one we went in. Two minutes later, we came out—minus most of our hair.

When I sat in the barber's chair, I counted how many swipes it took for me to be absolutely bald. Thirty-seven swipes and the barber said, "Get up. Next."

I was traumatized! I hadn't been bald since I was a baby. I got back in formation on this very hot August day only to be the center of attention.

It was all because I was now bald. When I got back in formation, the wind was blowing, and having never been bald, the wind felt like somebody was touching my head. I instinctively ducked. The TI saw me duck and came over and began yelling in my face. As he was yelling, the wind blew again, and I ducked again. Another TI saw it and came over. Now I had two of them yelling into my face.

What a great start. Later that night when I finally got to bed; it all started over. For the first time, I had head on pillow, no hair in between. Suffice it to say, I got very little sleep that night.

As our TI's were giving us the Do's and Don'ts, they mentioned that they would now find out who had a going away party, and who got thrown out of town when they left home. With that, they gave us our new mailing address, and I immediately sent mine out to all my friends and family. At the first mail call, I received several letters and packages.

This started happening on a daily basis and the TI asked, "Elder, did you have a going away party when you left home?"

And I replied, "Yes Sir, a huge one." He said, "That's obvious."

Not even two weeks into Basic Training my TI said, "Elder, report to the First Sergeant's Office."

I was terrified! How does the First Sergeant even know me and what does he want with me? When I reported, he asked, "When was the last time you wrote a letter home?"

I told him I thought I'd written last week. He said, "Sit down and write a letter to your mother right now!"

It turned out that my mother had called the Red Cross and told them she had not heard from me in a while. I was sitting there with my mouth wide open like, "WHAT?"

I continued to write the letter. I was sure to never let anything like that happen again. Mom wasn't playing, she was for real missing her baby boy.

Prior to going to Basic Training, I began to work out some to ensure I was in good physical condition. I would later learn that the Air Force Physical Training (PT) was a joke. We did very few pushups, sit-ups and only ran up to a mile and a half. I was eating three meals a day which I was not accustomed to, and I actually gained weight. I got to be a Squad Leader, and even earned a ribbon for my uniform as a Marksman for excellent rifle shooting.

Basic Training seemed to go by really fast and was quite easy once I learned that their goal was for us to work together and perform as a team. I even got the Air Force job that I wanted, Fire Protection.

Orders to United States Air Force in Europe (USAFE) "Germany."

After basic training, I was assigned to Chanute AFB, in Illinois for my technical school training. I was going into the fire protection career field, training to become a fire fighter. Chanute AFB was located near the small town of Rantoul, IL. There was nothing out there except a lot of corn fields. We had to march around those corn fields every morning and afternoon going to and from class. Of course, it was typical cold weather in Illinois from October through November. So those daily marches were no fun.

I had no idea when I signed up for fire protection that it was so technical. You can't just go in and put a bunch of water on a fire and think you are done. There is a science involved. Who knew? I had to learn the weight of water and what water does when it encountered heat. It began with learning the basic elements of the fire triangle which are "heat, oxygen and fuel." You need those three to have fire. Being a military fire fighter meant not only putting out fires in buildings but also in aerospace vehicles. We had to learn all about structures and aircrafts. This was fascinating for me. I will never forget the first time I went into a pit fire—a mock aircraft was ignited with jet fuel (JP4) and we had to walk in and extinguish the fire.

As in basic training, I met some really good people at Tech School and managed to keep in touch many of them. Jess Crothers who was in the same flight at basic training, was also at Chanute. He was there for Jet Engine Mechanic which was right next to the Fire Protection School. We continued our friendship. Jess even went roller-skating with me. For him it was just something to do, but for me Boogie Skating was not only my passion but now, it was a stress reliever. The rink was near the University of Illinois, the Fighting Illini and college chicks. Jess and I were having the time of our life.

One of my most memorable experiences at tech school was one day my roommate and I went to the post office. This was near the end of training when everyone begins looking for Permanente Change of Station (PCS) orders for your first duty assignment. When I opened my mailbox, I saw the big manila folder. My orders had arrived. I immediately opened it, and the first thing I saw was a blue packet that said, "United States Air Force in Europe (USAFE)."

My heart and head sank, and I dropped the envelope and walked away. My first assignment was going to be in Germany. This was just a short time after the Oktoberfest bombing that took place in Germany. Not to mention that I would have to be so far away from home and was thinking of how this would affect my mother. My head was spinning. My roommate picked up my orders and brought them back to our room. Once I calmed down, I looked over my package and tried to find the silver lining. Many of my other friends received orders to Germany also.

An Airman's Story: Coming Home to Leave

Tech School ended and we all graduated. Now, it was off to the new world of being in the Air Force. I had a flight scheduled from Chicago to Buffalo. By the time my bus got me to Chicago, I was a little pressed for time to make my flight. I had to take a taxi from the bus station to the airport. I met two brand new Navy recruits and they were heading to the same place, so we decided to catch a taxi together.

Once we got in, I told the driver that we were all pressed for time to get to the airport. Never tell a Chicago Taxi Driver that you are in a hurry. The driver pulled off so fast that we all had to turn around and get our hats off the back window. Thanks to the Chicago Taxi driver, we all made it in time for our flights, with time to spare.

—

My first homecoming as an Airman was outstanding. Everybody was so happy to see me, short hair, and all. The military had also helped me lose a few of those unwanted pounds. I had started doing pushups at Tech School, so my chest and arms looked great.

I got to hang out at all our regular spots and ate some of the best food in the world. The pizza, wings and hot beef on wick all from Western NY, were always the best. The highlight for me, though, was visiting the Carousel Skating Center. I couldn't wait to get there. I had to see who now thought they were the best skater, and check on the drama of the day, like who was dating who. In all, it was a great time but short lived. Before I knew it, it was time for me to leave for my new assignment in Germany.

1980 was the first time I'd spent Christmas away from home. December 22, 1980, just three days before Christmas was the actual date I departed for Germany. My mom and dad took me to the airport in Buffalo. There I was, in my dress uniform with slick sleeves "meaning no stripes" and all. My parents walked me to the airplane, and the closer we got, the harder my mom squeezed my hand. Finally, the time came to say goodbye. Not only my mom and dad, but this airman was crying, too.

I didn't want to go, but knew that I had to. I gave my dad a hug and kissed my mom, before walking onto the plane sobbing. At that moment, I realized I was now a young man and no longer the little boy who roller-skated at the Carousel. I was heading out into the world to make my mark. The flight attendants were so moved by our display of emotion that they pampered me to no end right till the time I walked off the airplane in New York City.

This would be my first International flight—a Pan Am 747 flight from NY to Frankfort, West Germany. We spent nearly eight hours on that plane. I didn't get pampered on that flight since the plane was full. I was somewhat afraid of flying so I pretty much stayed awake the entire flight. By the time we arrived in Frankfort, I was exhausted. I had to find my way to the bus terminal for my bus trip to Sembach Air Base (AB) which was about a forty-five-minute ride.

By the time the bus arrived at Sembach, I could barely keep my eyes open. They dropped us off at the Billeting Office where I received my room assignment. I proceeded to Barracks 212, room 320. Not long after I got to my room, Fred McGuire came down to welcome me. Fred and I had met at Tech School at Chanute and formed a friendship when we learned we would both be assigned at Sembach. We talked a while before he left, then minutes later, as I fell in and out of consciousness I asked myself: *Who was that?*

Welcome to Jet Lag! Fred and I laughed about that many times, afterwards. He said he saw me going in and out and remembered

when he first arrived and how he felt.

So, there I was two days before Christmas, all alone in a Country thousands of miles away from home.

Being home sick and fighting jet lag is a horrible combination. But the sleep was good. When I finally came out of my coma, one of my new Fire Department Assistant Chiefs invited Fred and me to his home for a Christmas Dinner with him and his family. That helped a lot. I wouldn't have to be alone on Christmas. This assignment, to

Firemen CJ Allen, Fred and Jeff

my amazement, was going to be the time of a lifetime. Just imagine, I was an 18-year-old young man living in another Country. I didn't have to worry about my food or paying for a place to live. All of those things were taken care of for me. I just had to enjoy myself, and beginning that day, I did.

The Base Sembach, consisted of two parts, the flight line area and the main base area. The fire station on the flight line was mostly for Aerospace vehicles and the buildings on the flight line. I was assigned to the 601st Civil Engineering

Squadron (CES). The flight line fire station was located in the same building as Base Operations and the Control Tower. Most of our rooms were on the third floor, which meant we had a fire pole to slide down when responding to emergencies. We had a great time with that pole, and yes, a few injuries since it was a three story drop. We had to be taught how to use it and not abuse it.

A week after getting to Germany, it was New Year's Eve. A lot of us signed up for the Mystery Train, a party train that took you to a secret location to bring in the New Year. After partying there for a while, it would bring you back to the base. This train took us to a location in France.

A strange thing happened to me on the train. I was going from one compartment to another, and passed a guy that I knew from high school. Lew Blevins graduated a year before I did. I knew he had joined the Air Force, but I didn't know he was stationed in Germany. It was truly amazing, being so far away from the U.S and seeing someone from my high school. But that was just the beginning.

Germany was looking a lot better every day. Its central location in Europe made it easy to travel on the weekends. The Ticket & Tours Office on base made sure the military members always had something exciting to do, so we wouldn't just sit in our dorm rooms drinking. At that time, no passport was needed for military members. A signed Form 80 allowed us access to several countries.

Any weekend I had free, I was on the move. In January I went skiing in the Black Forest. This was a huge change from skiing near Buffalo, NY. The weather was really nice and the only reason I needed snow pants was because I spent so much time on the ground. I wasn't the greatest skier, but I sure had a great time out there. I also found a new drink that would keep me warm when out on the sloop's—Glühwein, a German/Austrian winter-holiday drink that most tourists know as an after-ski drink. Once you come in from the snow, it supposedly makes the drinker glow with warmth pretty quickly. The only problem: since you drink this wine warm, the alcohol goes to your head much quicker! It was recommended that you only drink it once you were finished skiing.

I also traveled to the Keukenhof in Holland which is one of the most beautiful gardens in the world. This was a sight to see. Millions of tulips, daffodils and hyacinths filled nearly 39 acres with color and fragrance. At first, I wasn't interested in this tour, but I am so glad that I changed my mind. My very favorite trip that year was my weekend in Paris, France. Yes, Paris in the Springtime. I booked a three-day tour to Paris for $49. This included travel on a luxury double decker tour bus; overnight in a three-star hotel with a continental breakfast and seeing points of interest such as the Eiffel Tower, The Louvre, Notre-Dame de Paris, Arc de Triomphe and Sacre-Coeur, and the Basilica of the Sacred Heart of Paris. When I was in high school studying the Humanities, I would question why we needed to know any of that. Well, it all came into play when I visited these sites in Paris. I developed a true appreciation for my teachers.

Not only the sites, but the bus trip itself was quite interesting. The whole night before, I'd studied from my "learn to speak French" booklet. I got to put it to use when we went to dinner. When my group agreed they wanted another bottle of wine I told them I would take care of it. I called over the waiter, Garçon, and told him we wanted to check the price of another bottle of wine. Everybody started clapping. I thought I had asked how much was the bottle of wine? The waiter looked at me strange. I asked again. He still had this puzzled look on his face.

Exasperated, I finally broke down and spoke in English, "Can you bring us another bottle of this wine?" The waiter simply said, "Okay." Everybody at the table started laughing. So much for my speaking French.

The next day we were touring Paris in a double decker bus, when we saw a McDonalds. We asked the driver to stop, so we could try out the Parisian McDonald. Most streets, I quickly noticed, were extremely narrow compared to U.S. streets. Our Tour Guide said he needed a few strong men, so we came forward to help out. To our amazement, he wanted us to move a car that was partially blocking the street we were traveling on. This wasn't just any car, but a Jaguar. We all lifted the car onto the sidewalk but before we could get back on the bus, the owner of the Jaguar came out of the salon and was yelling in French at us. Our guide had a few words with the woman who owned the jaguar before returning to the bus and continuing our tour.

I was able to take some outstanding pictures standing in front of the Eiffel Tower. While we were at the Louvre and I was looking at the Mona Lisa, I thought it was strange that they would not allow people to take pictures with flashes. Although they said not to, many people were taking them anyway. Someone would take one with a flash on one side and the officer would walk over to them, and then someone on the other side would take one. It was comical. I found Paris to be beautiful, but not the cleanest place in the world.

Everywhere you walked you had to ensure that you were not stepping in dog poop. I found that quite annoying.

Football Season in the Military

I was grateful I got so much touring done when I did. In August, I tried out for the base football team. This was almost like semi-pro football. I recalled that when I arrived in Germany and asked how people got to know other people, I was told to join the football team. I couldn't wait to become a Sembach Tiger.

Finally, the announcements came out, and I'd made the team, though getting on the starting lineup was another story. As had always been my strategy for competition, during practice, I went above and beyond. That got me noticed by the coaching staff. When they had us do up and downs, I would throw my body on the ground and jump right back up. The coaches loved it. That got me a position on the Special Teams. Practices were long and hard. After one extremely hard practice, I took off my helmet and one of the guys said I looked like Woodstock the bird because of my hair. That nickname stuck. In fact, they later started calling me Woody.

When the time came for us to run the forty-yard dash, I just knew I was one of the fastest players on the team. We all lined up and when the whistle blew, I was off and running. I looked back and many were behind me, all except this white guy blowing my doors off. He was what we called a "sleeper." Nobody knew who he was, just that he sure could run. I hurriedly got to know him, my competition. His name was Gerald Gallagor, and we'd later all him the "G-Man" because he could run really fast and hit like a ton of bricks.

The G-Man and I became the best of friends and spent a lot of time together.

I didn't learn until later that the football team was the base commander's special project and he took great pride in his team being the best. He even flew his helicopter to all the away games. I found out how he felt about the team because I missed a practice and the coach asked me why. I told him my boss in the fire department would not let me off. That same day, the fire chief was summoned to the base commanders office and scolded for not allowing me time to practice. The next morning at shift change the fire chief made an announcement to both shifts: "Airman Elder will be allowed time to practice and time to participate in all games and the fire department will support him in these endeavors." I was shocked, but at the same time happy that I would get to participate.

The Sembach Tigers' first scrimmage game was against the "Fighting Chickens" from Royal Air Force (RAF) Chicksands, England. Our Assistant Coach Ken Fears was feisty and energetic. He knew just what to do to get us fired up and came in to talk to us right before we went out on the field.

He started out by telling us how good we were, and that we are Tigers. He then pulled out of a bag a chicken, and said, "There is no way a chicken can beat a tiger." He then stuck his hand up the butt of the chicken and told us to rip them apart. "Now, go and get them," he roared. Coach Fears had us so fired up we went out and beat Chicksands 47–7.

That motivation kept us going to our next scrimmage game which was a semi-pro team called the Manheim Redskins. We beat them 41–0. At this point, we thought there was no one who could stop us. Well, we were wrong, or maybe we just got the big head. We lost our first regular season game and went on to a mediocre season.

A couple of games into the season, Jerome Epps, the starting safety went down. The Coach called for me, "Elder!" I ran up and he told me, "You're in."

I said, "Coach, I'm not sitting on the bench anymore." And that was my big break. I never sat on the bench again. I was in excellent physical condition. I would jog with LC Hamilton who played on the team but was also a boxer. I would wrestle with the wrestling team with a fellow football player Terry Barret, who was the coach of the wrestling team.

Military Racquetball & Football

One day in the gym I was looking for some other workout when I saw a person come out of the racquetball court really sweating hard. I asked, "What is that?" They told me it was "racquetball." Of course, I had to check it out, see what it was all about and how they got to sweat that much. I went on the court, played, and had a wonderful time. I also got a very good workout out of it. Little did I know that this would be a new beginning for me. I was meeting a lot of people and having a good time.

Germany was turning out to be a great assignment. I was getting to roller-skate regularly because there was a roller-rink on Ramstein AB, only 20 minutes from Sembach. I would just go to the gate, push the share ride tab for Ramstein and anybody going that way would give me a ride. I would do the same to return to Sembach.

Sunday, August 30, 1981. The thought of the date still gives me chills. I remember exactly what I was doing that evening—skating at Ramstein. I had later returned to Sembach as I'd done dozens of times before. The very next morning there was a massive car bomb that exploded in the parking lot outside the USAFE headquarters building on Ramstein Air Base. Twelve U.S. Military members and two German civilians were injured. The German terrorist group, the Red Army Faction, later claimed responsibility for the attack. Just hours before, I had been on that base in the very same area.

As a firefighter at a nearby base, we were put on alert in the event we needed to respond for Mutual Aid to assist. My mom heard that a bombing happened at a US Air Base in Germany. She was excited, scared and desperately trying to get in touch with me. I called her as soon as I could, to reassure her that I was just fine. I knew several of the firefighters on Ramstein and one of them I knew from Tech School at Chanute. They all did a great job in responding to that event and received decorations for their bravery.

My regular Assistant Chief was Calvin J. Allen. He was married to a German National and he and his family would include me in many of their family events. I would get away from the Base and spend quite a lot of time with them. He spoke fluent German, and that inspired me to learn more.

Truthfully, I wanted to learn because I wanted to talk to the German girls.

I went to a club called the Blue Light and saw a very good-looking young lady. I asked her to dance, and she replied "nicht ferstein," which meant she didn't understand what I had said. I had thought all Germans understood English. I just said, Ok, and went about my business. I then took a crash course in German and returned to the club a few weeks later. When I saw the same young lady, I went up and asked if she would like to dance in German. She replied in English. "Oh, you speak German. I speak English."

Her name was Heide; and we not only danced that night, but also went on several dates. When I told her about our first meeting, later, she said that many Americans come over and only want to talk in English. They were more accepted if they at least try to speak the native language. I found that the farther away from the US bases you went, the more German dialects were spoken. If American service members at least tried to speak their language, they would put forward effort to communicate with you.

My supervisor Bradley D. Creasey and I would take road trips and was often invited into people's homes for lunch. After we ate lunch, they would always take a little cat nap. At first, we felt uncomfortable but later found ourselves joining right in. There is nothing like a good meal and a nap, to boot. One day on one of our trips, Brad's car broke down. I was overwhelmed by the German people's generosity.

Crowds of people stopped to help us, and we made some lasting contacts who we would later come back and visit.

Over time, I got tired of using share ride or bumming rides with Brad, so I looked into getting my own car. One of the civilian firefighters at Sembach had a vehicle for sale so I bought it. It was an Opel Ascona GT. After that, I was all over the place.

I was just 18 and not a big drinker when I was introduced to German beer. Not knowing how much stronger German beer was than American beer, I drank it much too fast and ended up quickly drunk. As for wine, Lambrusco was what I preferred, but later found out that German wine is outstanding. I totally stopped drinking beer because it was making me gain weight in my gut, and that was a no-no for someone who was passionate about staying in shape.

The football team would often go on a Wine Probe. Having my own vehicle meant that I wouldn't have to rely on others to bring wine back for me. We would go to several places and come back with trunks load of wine. Our football team could really drink. I was a light weight when it came to drinking, and I was fine with that.

As time went on, Gerald Gallagor and I did a lot of traveling together. We went to places like The Eagle's Nest in Berchtesgaden in Germany, the Salt Mines in Austria, and Bern, Lucerne and Interlaken in Switzerland—where people rowed around the lake in a boat. So, The G-Man and I rented a rowboat, though neither of us had ever rowed before. There we were, in the middle of the lake going around in a circle. People started looking and taking pictures of us. I guess it was a little funny. We finally got the hang of it and had a great time, while providing some entertainment for the real rowers.

During my second year as a Sembach Tiger I was voted as Special Teams Captain. The coach this year was an Air Force Academy graduate. He approached me about joining the Academy. I looked into it, was very interested and started the paperwork. But when I got close to signing those final papers, I opted out. The thing that really scared me was learning that if I did a year of Preparatory School, and three years regular, but somehow washed out, they would send me back to where I was in the military, at the same rank. I looked at the washout rate and decided that because I'd been out of the school scene for a while, it was best to stay where I was and continue my education on my own.

The Sembach AB Boosters would come to every football game, even the away games. They were very boisterous and would support us till the end, win or lose. When we traveled to away games half the team would ride home on the Booster bus. Well, that only happened one time. The coach put an end to what he called "such nonsense." They sure did know how to party though. We now had to wait till we got back home to join the party. It was always such a long bus ride back, especially after a victory.

The hardest I was ever hit was by my own teammate. Larry L. Livingston. He was our huge Middle Linebacker. Anytime the Defense would get an interception, the key word to turn around and block was "fire." So, when I got the interception, I yelled, "Fire!" And everybody turned and started blocking for me.

Well, there was a guy getting ready to tackle me and Larry was going to get him off of me. He yelled another key word "blue," which meant duck. When I heard blue, I ducked but I guess it was not quick enough. Larry hit both of us really hard. The medics had to come out with the stretcher for the guy that was trying to tackle me, and I limped off the field.

When we returned to our Base, I immediately reported to the hospital for x-rays and pain meds. When I left the hospital, I was wearing a neck brace and I went to the NCO Club to join the rest of the team. Larry apologized for hitting me so hard. I told him it was ok, but only because we won the game—thanks to my interception, I might add. We checked and the other guy was alright also, just a little sorer than I was. Our busters were at the club also, and I managed to get some special attention due to being in a neck brace.

There was another hard hit I remember quite well. It was a game against the Ramstein Rams. It was a very close game, and we were playing for the bragging rights in the Kaiserslautern area—better known as K-Town. I was playing the Monster Man position in that game which allowed me to choose which side of the field I played on.

This gave me an opportunity to get in on lots of tackles. This one tackle, however, I definitely could have done without. It was third down and we needed to get the ball back to have a chance to win the game. The Running Back, number 30 Gilesbie got the ball and hit the hole at the same time as I did. We met in a violent collision and we both fell backwards. He was stopped for no gain, and the whole stadium was in an uproar.

While my team was congratulating me for a great stop, they didn't know that I couldn't even breathe and wasn't quite sure of where I was. Yes, I saw stars and a few other things. I started running towards the sideline and hoping that it was the correct sideline when I saw my coach directing me back on the field to receive the punt. Really? I had just received the blow of a lifetime.

I gathered my faculties and got back out there for the punt. Being a defensive player, I loved to deliver a blow, but I could not stand for an opponent to try to hit me. It took everything that I had, but I managed to make a fair catch and evaded getting hit. I trotted off the field for some much- needed recoup time. Unfortunately, we lost that game and Ramstein had bragging rights yet again. Darn, that meant that I had to hear my best friend's brother Villo, who played on the Ramstein Rams talk smack.

Goodbye, Again

Being a member of the football team also meant that I got to know a lot of people around the base that could help out with special favors such as new assignments. I was within six months of my scheduled departure of Germany and needed to put in my Dream Sheet—my request for the Air Force Bases I wanted to go to. My friend at the Consolidated Base Personnel Office (CBPO), later renamed the Military Personnel Flight (MPF), asked me where I wanted to go for my next assignment. I told him I was from Niagara Falls, in New York. He said there was a base in Syracuse, NY but it would be deactivating in a couple of years. I immediately asked if he could still get me there, and it turned out that he could.

When I first arrived in Germany, one of the first things we young military members did was to get a Deferred Payment Plan (DPP) Card. This was our military credit card we used to charge at the Base Exchange for stereo equipment and other items. Many of the guys bragged that when they left Germany, they'd have the best stereo system money could buy. Others said they would have the best car. I bragged that I would have both—the best stereo and best car when I returned to "the world," the name we affectionately called the United States.

I had enjoyed my time in Germany and gave some thought about extending my tour there. But I didn't think about it in time. I was within six months of departure, and most likely my orders were in the system. I just knew I had to finish up whatever it was that I wanted to do before leaving Germany.

Gerald, the "G-Man," and I went on a few more tours. Most of the football team went to Bad Durkheim, which was the largest wine festival in the world. We had no clue what we were getting into. The Bad Dürkheim Wine Festival is over 500 years old and took place in the middle of town right outside the famous giant Wine cask (Dürkheimer Riesenfass)—the largest wine barrel in the world, which also houses a restaurant.

There were over 150 different wines just from the Bad Dürkheim region, in 50 different places throughout the fest. I think we tried them all. There was even a beer hall for those who prefer the grain to the grape! I was all about the wine. When we first arrived, we all purchased wine glasses, not just any wine glasses, but huge—different from any I had ever seen. As you continued to enjoy the festival, you continued to refill your glass. There were also little toy hammers with cushioned noise makers on each end and people would walk around hitting you on the head with them. After about half an hour of walking around drinking wine and getting hit with those hammers, we acquired the miniature hammers and started returning the favor. Thank goodness we all had hotel rooms because none of us would have made it back in one piece.

Fortunately, or unfortunately, most of my stories from Germany involve drinking. Lots of drinking. No question, the football team loved to party. One party was at Rob Lewis's house. He lived in the Sembach Base Housing area. Most of the team was there and we all had an outstanding time. When it was time for me to get a ride back to my barracks, Rob told me to come back over tomorrow for dinner and gave me his address: 76 C5. I asked him, "How the heck am I going to remember your address?" I started thinking: *76, that is the Bicentennial year and C-5; well that is the aircraft C-5 Galaxy. Ok, Bicentennial Galaxy.*

The next morning when I woke up, I was asking myself: *What the heck is Bicentennial Galaxy*? In time, I remembered Rob's address. He was extremely impressed that I made it to dinner on time. I told him the story of how I remembered his address and we were all in stiches laughing about it.

Unfortunately, about that time in June of 1982, I found out that my beloved Carousel Skating Center was closing its doors for good. Being so far away, I wouldn't even get to go to the final skating session. No more would I get to skate at the place that kept me out of trouble and off the streets while growing up. The Carousel was the place where I met so many friends, many of which became lifelong friends. It was also the place where I received my first real kiss. I had so many wonderful memories of the Carousel and felt blessed that I had the time there that I did. I am also glad I had already left Niagara Falls when it closed. I'm not sure what I would have done to fill the void. The Carousel's motto was "The Carousel Skating Center, where you bump into the best people." That was so true.

Ed Murray waving goodbye for last time

In my last game as a Sembach Tiger, Coach Meeker made me a bet. He said that he would buy my banquet ticket for me and a date if I would make the first tackle on kickoff. Each person on the kickoff team had an assignment and had to protect their lanes. I was the Headhunter and went straight to where the ball was. He always wanted to challenge me, and I was up for the challenge. As we kicked off the ball, I ran down the field like a mad man, possessed. I went straight to the ball carrier and delivered a blow that put him down. I then jumped up and shouted to Coach Meeker, "Dinner for two!" He smiled and told me to get back to work.

I had been trying to get a date with this one young lady for quite a while. Finally, I had a date set. I was in a great mood when I got off my shift in the Fire Department Communications Center AKA, the alarm room. I hurried to my dorm to shower and get ready and was walking to my room from the shower when the phone in the hall rang. I asked myself: *Do I answer this and take the chance that I will have to go look for somebody, or do I just go to my room and get ready?* I made the mistake of answering the phone. It was from the fire department and the call was for me.

The voice on the other end said, "Elder, you need to get back here to relieve Fred." Fred was being taken into custody for being under the influence of some narcotic, and they would explain the rest when I got there. I couldn't believe this was happening. I had finally got this date, and now I wouldn't be able to go. When I called her to explain, she wasn't interested in my excuse. At that point I knew that I had to just suck it up and return to work.

When I got there, I found out that Fred was high on some type of drugs. They questioned me about whether I'd noticed anything strange about his behavior. I had no clue that he was high and really all I was thinking about was getting back to get ready for my date. Fred was eventually kicked out of the military because of drug use. I felt really bad for him, he was a good guy and I enjoyed just listening to him talk smack.

Now that I had these tickets to the banquet, I thought: *This is my chance to approach her for another date.* I finally got up the nerve and asked. After some time, she said yes. I told her the date and time that I would pick her up. When I arrived to pick her up, she wasn't ready—not even close to being ready. I wondered if this was payback for my standing her up last time. Since I was one of the Team Captains, I had to be at the banquet early so I could sit on stage with the Coaches and the other Team Captains.

By the time we finally got there, the meal was being served. I felt totally humiliated, and we didn't get to sit on stage. I decided I had to make the best of it. All the team captains got to give a speech and when it came to me, I gave some inspiring words and the last thing that I said was something Coach Fears would always say. "No matter where you are in the world, when I say Sembach, you say Ha, when I say Sembach, you say Ha, when I say Sembach, you say Ha.

Break Down! Break Down! Break it all the way down, HA, HA, HA, HA!"

The crowd erupted, and my date was even a little impressed. As much as I'd wanted to take her on a date, this would be the one and only date I'd have with her.

Punctuality was always very important to me, and that evening had left a lot to be desired.

It turned out that my first cousin, Tommie was stationed in Germany during the same time. On one occasion, he actually came to visit me at Sembach. I was working the day he got on the Base area side, and my assistant chief suggested that he stay overnight at the fire station with us instead of going to billeting. This was outstanding, he not only got to spend more time with me, but he also had to endure sleeping in a bunk room with all the snoring... and, a few other noises all night.

In the morning we were awakened by the bells going off with an automatic alarm for building 141. Building 141 was the biggest building on the base and it was a Supply building. I was the fire truck driver for that shift. My cousin later told me he had laughed when he saw that the guys had barely got on the back of the truck before I was pulling out of the station. Back in those days we still rode on the back of the fire trucks. We had a buzzer to push to notify the driver that they were strapped in and ready to move. As soon as I heard the buzzer I was gone. As it turned out, the call was a false alarm. Unfortunately, that was nothing unusual.

The time had come for me to tie up all lose ends and prepare for my departure from Germany. I had an outstanding stereo system that I considered the best of the best. I had the PLL-1000A all linear Turntable; the GFX66R Duel Cassette Player; the Akai 747 Reel to Reel; the Bose 901 Speakers and it was all powered by the KR1000 Receiver and Tuner.

Now, I just needed to get my automobile to take back to the World. It didn't take long, a Non-Commissioned Officer (NCO) had a car posted on the Post Office wall and he was PCS-ing soon. I went to look at the car and immediately loved it. It was a 1979 Volvo 242DL. That was the safest car on the road in 1979. It was fast and came in my favorite color, Candy Apple Red. I mentally claimed it, but just had to get all of my financing together. I sold my Opel to G-Man and sold a few pieces of my stereo system. This way, I was leaving Germany with a great stereo system and an outstanding automobile.

As would be expected, my tour of duty didn't go by without a little scandal. Not necessarily involving me but almost the entire fire department. There was a pay phone in the hall down near the entrance to the building. Somehow, somebody found out the coins would get stuck, and you could make unlimited calls all over the world. Things were cool at first, but then people started fighting over who could use the phone next. The Air Force Office of Special Investigation (OSI) got involved and an investigation got

under way. Everybody got called in. The investigation team even wanted to question the German Nationals, but they were out of their jurisdiction. All the military in the fire department got some sort of action taken against them except for two Airmen. I happened to have been one of those two lucky souls.

Within no time at all, I received PCS Order to report No Later Than (NLT) date of 7 January 1983, to the 4789th Air Base Group (ABG) in Hancock Field, North Syracuse, NY. I was elated. I was going home or at least, near home. From the Base to my mother's driveway was 153 miles. I know because I drove it almost every other weekend. In the fire department we had a thing called a "Kelly-Day," or K-Day for short. We would work twenty-four hours on, then have twenty-four hours off. Every other week we would get three days in a row off. My K-Day was Saturday. So that meant that I was off every Saturday.

Part Three

U.S. Air Force Civil Service

Back to the World

I arrived at Hancock Field on Friday, January 7, 1983, my "Report No Later Than" date. I received my temporary dorm room and was shown where all the base facilities were. That night, while falling in and out of deep sleep, I had the radio on and heard an advertisement for a roller- rink. Not fully understanding what was said, the next day I grabbed my roller-skates and proceeded out to find this rink. All I knew was Brewerton. So, I pulled out my map and saw Brewerton on the map and drove there. After searching for hours, I was not able to locate the rink.

I finally gave up and decided to return to the base, but I noticed that driving back seemed longer than before so I thought I must have missed my turn. I decided to turn around at the next entrance. When I pulled in the parking lot, I looked up and saw Sports-O-Rama, then I saw roller- skating rink. I could not have planned this in a million years. I found a roller-skating rink. I went in and could not wait to get my skates on. As soon as I got in there, people were checking me out. A guy named Rick looked suspiciously at me before approaching me and asking where I was from. I told him Niagara Fall, but I was stationed at Hancock Field. He was suddenly okay and started introducing me to his friends.

It turned out the rink was like a soap opera, and in no time, I became the starring character. Being an avid skater and having a totally different style, everybody wanted to know how I was doing the things that I do. I was happy to share.

That's where it all began. Rick was a very good speed skater and I was a very good Boogie skater, so we helped each other learn. It also helped that Rick knew everybody. We started hanging out all the time. I enjoyed visiting him at his home, except for the huge

Doberman Pincher that I wasn't sure liked me. I tried to keep my distance from him.

Visiting Rick was a relief from dorm life. My dorm was in barracks 222, in room 222. I always said, "Good things happen in the 2's." I was very fortunate to even get this room. Most of the dorm rooms shared a bathroom, but mine had its own bath. It just so happened that a friend who worked in the fire department had lived there before me. When he was leaving the military, he had me move some of my things in, so when it came time for me to move in, I could naturally claim the room as mine.

With my K-Day being Saturday I was able to leave for Niagara Falls when I got off on Thursday morning, and returned to the base for skating on Saturday night—the best night. It was during one of those nights I met a red head named Dianna that lived near the base. I asked her if she needed a ride home. When she said no, I moved on.

Rick and I were out cruising one night when we came up to TJ's Big Boy a food joint. He saw one of his friends and called her over to introduce us. Her name was Ann. He told me later that she had wanted to meet me. Not much later, I began dating Ann. That was just the beginning of my dating fiascos while stationed in Syracuse. Our relationship lasted for a few months but when we broke up, I decided I needed to get away. It just so happened that a Temporary Duty Assignment (TDY) came up for a classified location.

I volunteered and was accepted.

The Sandbox Hotel

My desire to get away came soon. I received a 30-day temporary assignment to participate in exercise Bright Star, then was later moved up to exercise Prized Falcon which was for a minimum of 60 days. When I told mom I was going away for a minimum of 60 days to a classified location, she was very upset, but eventually got over it. I took my car home to Niagara Falls so that she could use it while I was gone. My car was a four-speed manual shift and my mom didn't know how to drive a manual shift, so I gave her a crash course and she managed.

Mom and dad brought me back to Hancock Field and I packed my bags. The first thing I packed was my roller- skates. Then I was off to Hill AFB in Utah, our staging area. Once there, we received additional equipment and shots and boarded a C-5 Galaxy Aircraft heading Overseas. By that point we all knew we were heading to Egypt which was going to be an extremely long flight. At that point I was thinking: My skates will get absolutely no use. A couple hours into flight, the crew said we were experiencing some difficulties, and we'd have to land at Dover AFB in Delaware. It looked as if we would have to spend the night, or at least until repairs were made.

When we arrived at Dover, we boarded a bus for the Billeting office. As we were riding, I looked out the window and saw someone walking that I knew from Sembach. I yelled out to him, and it turned out I was able to spend a few hours with him and his family before I had to report back to the aircraft. I thought that was really cool.

It didn't take long for the aircraft to be repaired. We all loaded back on and took off from Dover, for Egypt— another extremely long flight. Immediately after landing in Egypt, Cairo West, we were whisked off to a hotel. Not just any hotel. This was the El Salem Hyatt Hotel. The same hotel that former Presidents Carter and Reagan stayed in when they were in Egypt for the funeral of Former Egyptian President Anwar Sadat. Five Star all the way. There were two people per room but living like this it was well worth having a roomie.

After a nearly twenty-hour day trip, we were all severely jet lagged. Once I found my room I didn't even unpack, just fell on the bed. Just a few minutes later I heard what sounded like somebody saying "Fire. Fire!" I thought I was dreaming until I looked at my roommate, and he heard it too. Well, when a fireman hears the word "fire," they automatically proceed to where it is. That is just what I did.

I had all of my fireman gear with me in my Mobility Bag (MOB), and I quickly donned it and ran down the hall. Once I got there I was met by other firemen. We immediately began doing what we do—fighting the fire. Another fireman and I had the fire pretty much knocked down when somebody pulled the blanket off the bed. The room immediately flashed over and was fully engulfed again.

Those at the door were forced out and the two of us were trapped near the balcony. Because we were on the third floor, there was no escape. Without hesitation, I ran through the fire and grabbed the hose and was able to knock down the fire again so that my new friend could escape.

The fire had been contained to just that one room. The hotel management and staff were very appreciative for our heroic acts. From that point forward, we were their honored guest. They treated us like celebrities, and thew us a huge thank you celebration by the pool. We later found out what caused the fire—

a British Airways Flight Attendant had been smoking in bed and fell asleep.

Army Brigadier General Musser was also a resident at the hotel and witnessed our heroic acts. He recommended that all Airman involved in this incident be put in for the Airman's Medal. This action was to be followed up by our respective bases, once we returned from the TDY. As it turned out, there was a mix up and the order was never sent to our Bases. None of us received the Medal.

As a fire fighter, we were accustomed to working every other day, so we kept that same schedule over there. Every morning it was more than an hour's ride to get to the base which was out in the middle of the desert. On our days off we would hang out by the pool, lift weights and play cards. I got in excellent condition on that TDY. I was even able to use my roller-skates, after all. The Hotel had a talent night and I got on stage and performed some of my routines. The crowd was quite amazed—first, that I could do those things on skates, and second, that I even had skates in Egypt, in a country of deserts.

We found out the participants of the exercise, Bright Star, was in Tent City in the Desert, and Prized Falcon was in a five-star hotel. On the weekends, Bright Star participants could visit our hotel to swim and relax. I was very happy that I was moved up to Prized Falcon.

While we were there, I formed a close relationship with the hotel's food and beverage manager, Gamel, who was a great friend to have. He would take me out to places that I most definitely would not have gone to all alone. He was always there to get my drinks at Vito's, the club located in the international lounge on the lower level of the hotel. As a group we went out touring, and because of Gamel, I was able to see some of the wonders of the world. We rode camels in the desert—right up to the Pyramids in Giza. We saw the Sphinx and even took a dinner cruise along the famous Nile River. One of the most exciting sites for me was a museum we visited in Egypt. It was just amazing to think that our history is just a little over 200 years old while Egypt's history is thousands of years old. I was truly thankful for the opportunity to see that history.

Each day, flight crews would come into the hotel from Ward Air of Canada, Air France, Egypt Air and Lufthansa from Germany. Of course, all of us military guys would post up to see who we could talk to. I always gravitated to the Lufthansa crews because I spoke some German.

One evening our bus was late coming back from the desert and everybody was already in Vito's. When I arrived, I saw all my guys, then I looked over and saw two good looking women sitting at the bar. There was one empty seat next to them. I looked at my guys again, then made a b line to the empty seat at the bar. When I got there, Gamel had a drink waiting for me. There was always good music in Vito's, and I overheard the ladies saying, "You should get up and dance."

I politely leaned over and asked if one of them would like to dance. The young lady by the name of Anya said yes. Now my buddies were looking over at me, wondering how was it that I walked in and secured a dance partner that quickly.

They later told me they were preparing to make a move when I came along and beat them to it. "All I saw was an empty seat and an opportunity," I told them.

One night the hotel threw a DJ competition. I had brought lots of different kinds of music with me, so I signed up for the competition. There was only a few of us that signed up for it. I was on first. I started with the hand clap of Kano, I'm ready. That got the crowd started and I had them eating out of my hand until my set ended. The crowd and hotel management were the judges. When it was all done, I was crowned as the winner. My prize was a free weekend stay at any Hyatt hotel in the world. I just had to pay to get to the location. Not bad for playing some music and having a good time.

The days in the desert were hot and long. As a firefighter, there was not much going on, so we spent most of our time writing letters to those back in the World, working out and playing cards. That is where I learned how to play Bid Whist. I had a loyal group of pin pals that I had to keep in touch with, since I would be going back to Syracuse. At work we would use the sun to heat up our food. Meals Ready to Eat (MRE's). MRE's were not the most tasty and nutritious food but in a pinch, they filled the void of hunger. At the hotel we were getting full per diem and could order whatever we wanted to eat and have our clothing laundered. We also got to do some outstanding shopping as a huge outdoor shopping area was nearby. It was called Khan Al-Khalili. This was a massive shopping area where you could barter for whatever you wanted. But all good things must come to an end.

An Airman's Dream: Skating and Dianna

The time came for us to load up and head back to our bases. When I arrived back at Hancock Field by way of Niagara Falls to pick up my car, I was surprised, but grateful that it had survived my mother's driving. I couldn't wait to go roller-skating at Sports-O-Rama and tell everyone about my many adventures in Egypt. I also had to follow up on some of those faithful pen pals. It didn't take me long at all to get right back in the groove of things both at work and play. I saw that fiery redhead again and she finally started giving me a second look, but she still wouldn't let me give her a ride home.

Since leaving, my popularity at the rink soared. I joined Rick's speeds skating Team. I was impressed that he was also team captain. For me, skating came easy, but the endurance needed to speed skate was a totally new venture. I was very fast out of the blocks, but others would soon catch up until I learned to master those new speed skates. When I first started speed skating, I tried to use my Micro Stars, but they were far too heavy. That meant I had to purchase some ultralight speed skates. That wasn't the problem, I had to get used to them and that took some time. But when I did get used to them, I was a force to be reckoned with.

Many of my faithful pen pals wanted to start hanging out with me so I hardly ever had any time for just me. One night the red head asked me if I could give her a ride home.

Unfortunately, I already had plans and was not able to. I guess that was all it took, she started pursuing me. The first time we went out was for ice cream at Friendly's, where most everyone from the rink hung out. I must have made a good impression because she invited me over to her house for Christmas dinner with her whole family.

As it turned out I was scheduled to work on Christmas, but I asked my boss if I could take some time off and go to the dinner. He said, yes. I went over in my uniform, but to my surprise when I got there, she introduced me to her boyfriend. WHAT? Boyfriend? Awkward! She then let me know that her parents liked this guy and invited him, but I was her special guest. His name was Cliff. That reminded me of a book that I had when I was a child called *Clifford the Big red Dog*, so I called him "The Big Red Dog." That Christmas was Cliff's last dinner. Dianna and I started dating, and that was it.

—

I was an avid racquetball player, and I met someone who was my match in racquetball. Nevador was older and married. His wife was Carolyn. They had two children Denedra and Nevador, Jr., who we all called Nevie. The family often invited me over for dinner. Both Nevador and I had a very competitive edge so we would try to outdo each other every time we played racquetball. Those times were great, but there was this other guy who gave me fits on the racquetball court. His name was Chuck. Chuck was lanky and could move really well on the court. To top it off, he liked to talk smack just like I did, and we instantly got along. I just had to find a way to beat him consistently. Well, that never happened but we had a great time going back and forth. Chuck and I eventually played for the Base Racquetball Championships. He won, but he allowed me to take the three-foot trophy home.

Because Hancock Field was such a small base, I was allowed to take one of the fire trucks to the gym while I worked out. If we had a response while I was there, I would respond from the gym. We were all over the place with those fire trucks. Membership had its privileges.

After being on Hancock Field for a year, the Tactical Air Command

(TAC) Assessment Team which is responsible for assignments for a closing base came in and told me that that they would send me to any TAC base I wanted to go to. I knew when I arrived at Hancock Field that it would only be a very short assignment, so after a year in the cold and snow of Syracuse, I looked on the TAC map and saw Homestead, South of Miami and said, "That is where I want to go." My next Base was set. I was going to Homestead AFB in South Florida. I would get to stay at Hancock until the day of de-activation which was June 30, 1984.

That last six months seemed to go by in a flash. However, before I left Hancock Field, I served briefly as acting base fire chief for the last period of operations. Before I knew it, the time had come for me to pack up my things and leave North Syracuse. I proceeded to Niagara Falls to spend time with my family before heading to Florida. I also spent a lot of time going back and forth from Niagara Falls to Syracuse. You would think that having only been at Hancock Field for a year and a half that I would not have any ties to the area. Not so. Let's just say that red was my favorite color and that it might just have caused me to come back a time or two.

In the middle of July, I packed my Volvo in Niagara Falls and left for my new assignment at Homestead AFB in Florida.

My first overnight stop was going to be at my Aunt Versie and Uncle Jimmy's house in Atlanta, Georgia. My cousin Felecia from Niagara Falls was going to Florida A&M for Nursing but was headed to Atlanta first. My Aunt and Uncle would take her to the school. It was convenient for her to ride to Atlanta with me.

This was my cousin's first time away from home and it made me remember the first time I left home. There was a lot of crying at her house, and it took us a while to get out of there. The ride was at least seventeen hours from Niagara Falls to Atlanta and it was nice to have company. We played backgammon along the way and she got a good laugh when I got pulled over in Ohio for speeding. At the time she was extremely silent but later she told me that she was cracking up on the inside. I had the butter face because I just could not believe that it had happened. The silence only lasted so long, and we were back to talking and playing backgammon. We arrived in Atlanta with no other incidents, thank goodness.

We woke up the next morning to my Aunt's wonderful breakfast. I said my goodbyes and continued my ride to Homestead—all the way to the bottom of Florida. I would be on the road at least another eleven or twelve hours. I had no idea that Florida was so long. Finally, I made it to Homestead and checked into Billeting.

Homestead AFB

Homestead was hot and humid in the middle of July. Unfortunately, my Volvo didn't have air conditioning and I had to just deal with the heat. This was not a real problem for me. After all that time in Syracuse with the snow, the heat was a welcome relief. After I did all of my in- processing, I reported to the Fire Station. I was met there by Steve, one of my co-workers who had been stationed at Hancock Field. As it turned out, several people stationed at Hancock Field was transferred and stationed at Homestead.

My good friend Nevador and his family had already arrived and lived in Base Housing. This was good for me because their house is where I spent most of my time to get away from the dormitory. I also got a surprise when I reported to the fire department. When my new boss asked me, "Where is your hometown?" I said Niagara Falls, New York. He said there was another guy there from Niagara Falls, and his name was Aquino. I asked, "Fred Aquino?" He said, yes, and called Fred in. We spent the afternoon reminiscing about our hometown.

—

For the next year I spent a lot of time either driving or flying back to Syracuse. That little red head (Dianna) and I had gotten serious. So serious that I had bought a ring set. My friend's wife Carolyn kept the ring in their safe for me and every time I would fly up to Syracuse, she would take me to the airport and before I got out of the car she would ask me if I wanted to take the ring with me. But I kept saying no. One time I was going up for Dianna's birthday and I told Carolyn I wanted to take the ring. When I got to Syracuse the time just didn't seem to be right for me so when

Dianna took me to the airport, I told her that I came to do something, but I didn't. I then got on the plane and returned to Homestead.

Not a month later I invited Dianna to Florida. We went to Key West, and I remember the sign that said, "Go all the way in Key West." So, that's exactly what I did. We went to the end of the pier just ninety miles from Cuba and I got down on one knee and proposed. Dianna was very surprised and immediately said yes. We were married in Niagara Falls, New York in December of 1985. Shortly after that we drove back to Homestead and moved into an apartment in South Miami Heights called the Cabana Club Apartments.

Nevador and Carolyn weren't able to make it to the wedding in Niagara Falls, so they hosted a wedding party at their home once we arrived in Homestead. I really owe them for looking out for me. The fact that Nevador was an officer, and I was enlisted made for strange friendships. You rarely saw the friendships between these two levels.

Nevador, though, was like my big brother and his family became my family. All of his brothers, sisters and even his parents treated me like family. One of the most special things about the military is the great friendships. I've met some of the greatest people in the world and formed friendships that have lasted a lifetime.

Fred Aquino was very instrumental in my becoming an active Christian. I was singing in the choir at the Base Chapel and very involved in the services, but Fred asked me if I had been baptized and if I wanted to come to church with him some day. He told me about his minister at Goulds Church of Christ, who he said was a dynamic speaker.

I agreed to go, and my wife and I attended. We both thought it was very different from the churches we'd visited, but we enjoyed ourselves. Not long after that we were both baptized into the Lords Body. Fred didn't stay at Homestead very long. He left the military and went back to school. He also became a minister and teacher. We saw each other in Niagara Falls a few times, and I even had him review a few bible lessons with my mother.

Life as a military fire fighter was not the most exciting thing. We got to ride around base always in a clean fire truck and did some good training, but we never got any business. Of course, In the big picture, that was a good thing. Things would, however, get busy when a Hurricane was forecasted to come our way. All fire fighters would have to assist, as all the bases' aircrafts would leave for safer areas. Then we would have to go around the base and remove coconuts from some of the trees as they could become flying projectiles. We would then have to hunker down and ride out the storm, all the while getting calls from residents that did not heed the evacuation warning and needed help. At a certain point we had to tell them they had to ride it out as we would put ourselves in too much danger to try and come out in the midst of a storm.

There were a few perks of the job. There was a need for rescue divers, and the state of Florida was willing to pay for all of the equipment and training for this certification. A few of us military firefighters jumped on this opportunity. We started off in the base pool and eventually ended up diving to a depth of 110 ft. at mile marker 86 in the Florida Keys which is Islamorada. I was spoiled instantly. Scuba diving in the only Natural Coral Reef in the Continental United States was outstanding. I never got to use the training in real life, but I did get Underwater Rescue Diver Certified.

Part Four

Performing on the Main Stage

Career Moves

When George H. W. Bush was Vice President, he would often vacation in the Florida Keys. When he did, his plane, Air Force Two (AF-2) would park in front of Base Operations, which was right next to the fire department. When this occurred, all fire department personnel would have to sit in our trucks just in case the Vice President wanted to stop by and greet us.

After the Vice President's motorcade zipped by, Charlie Zitzow, a civilian firefighter in my truck, said, "You see those guys in those nice three-piece suits?"

I said, "Yes."

And he replied, "They are Active Duty Air Force just like you are."

I looked at what they were wearing, then at what I was wearing, and said, "Why is it that they can go to work looking like that, and I go to work looking like this?"

I told him I was going out to talk to them and find out. I did just that, went out and introduced myself and inquired about their job. I was told that it was a special duty assignment and that they were flight attendants. I asked, "How do I sign up for something like this?" They referred me to the Consolidated Base Personnel Office (CBPO).

On Monday morning I was at CBPO getting all the pertinent information for a special duty assignment. Of course, I had to get supervisor approval, first. I also had to get letters of recommendation, pass a flight physical, and attend physiological training, just as a beginning. I knocked them all out in no time at all. After a short while I received a request for an interview. Master Sergeant Larry Adams came to Homestead to interview me. This was great for him as he had a daughter that lived in Miami and he was able to kill two birds with one stone. Once he completed his interview, he recommended me to interview at Andrews.

As I was going on leave and would pass right by Andrews AFB, I was granted an interview. When it was all said and done, my package was accepted and I received orders for a four year controlled tour to the Special Duty Assignment of Inflight Passenger Service Specialist (IPSS), at the 1st Military Airlift Squadron (MAS), which was part of the 89th Military Airlift Wing (MAW) at Andrews AFB in Maryland. My Report No Later Than date was July 22, 1987.

Nevador was in the middle of performing a one-year remote assignment to South Korea and he received follow- on orders to Langley AFB in Virginia. Langley is a three- hour drive from Andrews. You know this sat well with us as we had a very strong relationship. My report date was before his, so Dianna and I drove the Volvo up first and later came back for my other vehicle, the Datsun 280ZX, which I left at Nevador's house. I had a wonderful time living in South Florida and still have very fond memories of my days as a fire fighter. But I was ready for a change and here it comes. I was assigned a Sponsor and her name was Sheila. A sponsor helps you get acquainted to the base, local area and in processing.

—

When we arrived at Andrews AFB, we were driving two vehicles. I said to Dianna, "Welcome to our home for the next four years." As it turned out, however I was at Andrews just shy of 20 years.

Sheila was there to greet us and get us started. We lived in Temporary Living Facility (TLF) until our apartment was ready.

When it was ready, we moved to Fort Washington, Maryland—just eight miles away from the Base. Once I was processed in at Andrews, I started training immediately as an In-flight Passenger Service Specialist (IPSS).

The Squadron was the 1st MAS, and it consisted of big birds (VC-137C and the VC-135) and small birds (VC-9C and VC- 20). Most of the training we received was as an IPSS, was hands on from the many instructors in the squadron. Many of the instructors were duel qualified for both big and small birds. The first thing I had to learn was about the heritage and history of the 89th Military Airlift Wing Special Air Missions (SAM) which is founded on the principles of excellence; and what was SAM Fox. The wing is now the 89th Airlift Wing, under the Air Mobility Command, which is part of the United States Transportation Command.

I soon learned that the 89th Airlift Wing's primary mission is to transport the President of the United States aboard "Air Force One." In addition, the Wing is tasked to provide safe, reliable and comfortable worldwide airlift for the Vice President, Cabinet members, members of Congress, military leaders, and other high-ranking dignitaries of both the United States and foreign governments. Some of the most famous and powerful people in the world had traveled aboard 89th aircraft.

These experiences and sincere commitment to the SAM FOX style of job performance is what distinguishes the 89th crew member from any other in the world. "SAM FOX" had come to denote an attitude of extraordinary professionalism and dedication to perfection—an ideal that continues to be the primary objective of the personnel assigned to the 89th Airlift Wing. I was selected to immediately start training on one of the small birds called the VC-9C. The VC-9C was a decked-out DC-9. The interior was orange and brown and I recall thinking: *This is the coolest plane I have ever been on.*

Because of fuel range limitations, the aircraft was selected for Special Air Missions in North and South America. My first flight was on August 23 – 28, 1987. As it turned out, Sheila's soon to be husband, John, was the Flight Mechanic on that crew. The flight crew consisted of two pilots, one flight mechanic, and four flight attendants. Our Distinguished Visitor (DV) on the aircraft was Carl E. Vuono, the Four-Star General who served as the Chief of Staff (COS) of the United States Army. We flew from Andrews to Missouri, and then on to Central America.

My first Aircraft Commander was Lt. Col. Jessie Glisson. Knowing that this was my first flight in the 89th he pulled me to the side and gave me a rundown on the squadron and how things operated. He warned me that not all Aircraft commanders would be like him. I was fortunate to have had him as my first Aircraft Commander. He taught me a lot and I enjoyed his company. Lt. Col. Glisson even hooked me on his favorite musical group, *The Dire Straits* from Australia. My instructor, Tom Ryder, was infatuated with "The Grease Man," a local radio host on DC-101. I didn't really understand the humor, but I realized I was the new guy on the block and needed to be very adaptable. When we landed back at Andrews, I received a coin from the Army COS on my very first mission. I had a great first flight, but at the same time, I realized just how much I had to learn about this new flying career of IPSS.

Alaska, Korea & Colin Powell

One of my most memorable missions on the VC-9C was my first flight to Alaska. We were flying into Fair Banks, Alaska inside the Arctic Circle. Prior to the mission, the crew had to report to Base Supply's Individual Issue, where we were assigned Cold Weather Gear. Our DV for this mission was the Army General responsible for the Artic Exercise Brim Frost 1989. Little did I know that this mission would push the crew and everybody that participated in the exercise to the brink.

Operation Brim Frost 89 was to be the largest winter war games ever in Alaska. Unfortunately, this also turned out to be one of Alaska's most extreme winters with record cold spells which produced an official low of minus 76 degrees Fahrenheit. This was not a Wind Chill; this was the ambient temperature.

Governor Steve Cowper activated the state's emergency broadcast system, advising residents not to travel, to stay indoors and to keep warm. Another Alaskan Official was quoted as saying, "It's so cold the thermometer ran out of numbers." These extreme temperatures during the exercise claimed nine lives and contributed to some 253 cold weather injuries.

According to the World Almanac and Book of Facts, this is how dangerous below freezing temperatures are:

At -20, motor oil becomes a thick gel and will not move through the engine of a vehicle.

At -40, exposed flesh freezes within a minute. At -60, exposed flesh freezes within seconds.

At -60 or colder, breath turns to ice crystals that fall to the ground.

One of my crewmembers, Randy and I donned our cold weather gear and had to experience this cold weather for ourselves. We went out and had a cup of water in which we threw up in the air and it immediately crystalized. I managed to get a picture of this, and it turns out to be the last picture taken by this camera as it froze up and never worked again.

One can only imagine what it takes to keep an aircraft operational during such extreme conditions. Our crew had our hands full. We had to drain the aircraft of all water, remove any consumable liquids, and place some sort of heating source to each landing gear and into the fuselage. It was a lot of hard work, but most importantly, we managed to keep the aircraft up and running. When we returned to Andrews, our crew was nominated for the Military Airlift Command (MAC) Aircrew of the Year Award. We didn't win but it was a great honor to just be nominated.

My First Korea Visit

After getting fully qualified on the VC-9C, another mission came up. Each Squadron would provide an IPSS to fly Distinguished Visitors on other military aircrafts. For this particular mission, it was the late Greg Davis from the 1st Airlift Squadron and me, from the 99th on a C-141 Starlifter Aircraft, with a Silver Bullet comfort Pod. This Comfort Pod had all the conveniences of home and made traveling long distances much easier in what would normally be a long, cold and uncomfortable flight. The C-141 flight crew also enjoyed having IPSS's onboard, and they were delighted because we would treat them to the culinary services and conveniences as the DV. In other words, they were getting spoiled.

Our DV for this mission was General Gary E. Luck who was flying over to take Command of the United States Forces Korea. Flying from Andrews to Osan, Air Base in South Korea was an extremely long flight that required two in- flight refuels. This was a new experience for me as the aircrafts I had flown on before, had to land to refuel.

In 1988, South Korea hosted the XXIV Summer Olympic Games from September 17 – October 2. This mission was in June of 1988 and my first time going to South Korea. I soon I found out that the prices for goods had not gone up until right about the time of the Olympics. I was able to buy shoes, tailor made clothing and other items for remarkable prices. I was flying back on a C-141 aircraft, so I was not concerned with having enough space in my bags. I simply bought new ones. By the time we returned to Andrews, I had spent the fifteen hundred dollars I signed out for mission support and had all of my Christmas shopping completed for the year. Greg and I had an outstanding time getting to know each other. Mission accomplished.

C-20 Mission, and a Celebrity Experience

I began training on the C-20B which were Gulfstream III Aircrafts capable of flying around the world. The C-20B's normal crew component include five members: pilot, co- pilot flight engineer, communications systems operator and flight attendant. The plane has a range of 4,250 miles (3,698 nautical miles) and can hold up to 12 passengers for a max capacity of 18 total people. The C-20B is also capable of flying up to altitudes of around 45,000 feet. This aircraft could get up and go.

With the C-20B being worldwide, and me being a student, I got priority when it came to scheduling missions. I would get to go to some really great places, like Mazatlán, Mexico. My Instructor was none other than Gerald "Jerry" Von Monroe. Jerry was cool, and still sported an Afro and made it look good. Jerry gave me a nickname of "Dweeze." I have no idea where it came from. Our aircrew was set up to stay in villas on the beach for our time there. Once we got settled in, Jerry said let's go out to the beach. He ordered two of their famous coconut drinks, and when they arrived, Jerry said, "Dweeze, look around. We are getting paid for this." At that point, I knew I had made the right career decision.

As it turned out, I had Jerry as my instructor for many missions, including the first time I flew to Israel. Our DV was the late, Four Star General Maxwell Reid Thurman, the commander of United States Army Training and Doctrine Command at the time. General Thurman had been dubbed "Mad Max" by his colleagues. This was always a difficult mission; not necessarily because of the General, but his aide was a very demanding person. We thought he always looked to find something we could not do and demanded we do it. Let's just say he kept us on our toes.

After we arrived in Israel and got settled in our hotel, I was anxious to get out and see Tel Aviv. I had always heard how beautiful Israel was and now I was able to experience it for myself. I knocked on Jerry's door, then stretching out my arms and legs, I climbed up the wall. When Jerry answered the door, he looked down the hall both ways, then finally looked up at the ceiling and saw me. He laughed so hard he started crying.

After we composed ourselves, we went to an outdoor area and immediately noticed that people were looking at us and pointing. I thought it was because we were African Americans. Not exactly. A few of them were brave enough to approach us. They thought we were Richard Pryor and Eddie Murphy. We kept telling them no, we were not but they insisted that we were. We were not able to buy anything. Whatever we wanted they took care of. Finally, we gave in, and enjoyed ourselves. The rest of the mission went great, and Jerry recommended me for my C-20B evaluation flight.

—

My Once in a Lifetime Flight, with Colin Powell and the Jeff Burgers

After completing my training on the C-20B, which included my recommendation for an evaluation flight; my next flight would be my Check Ride. This would turn out to be one of my best flights during my time in the 99th Squadron. You see our DV was The General Colin Powell and his Aide. General Powell was a man that I truly admired and very much wanted to know more about. We were taking him to California, dropping them off and deadheading home.

My Flight Evaluator was the Late Bill Hartnett. MSgt Hartnett had a reputation for being an extremely hard evaluator. When I made contact, they said that the Chairman wanted burgers. I remembered that I had an excellent recipe for burgers where I would par cook them on my grill at home then finish them on the plane. I called them my "Jeff Burgers."

Things were going good on my check ride. When I served the Chairman, he took a bite then looked at the burger. He then took another bite and called me over. He said, "This burger."

I said, "Sir, is there something wrong?"

He said, "No. It's great." He then asked what was in it, and I hesitated.

He noticed my hesitation, and said, "Oh, chef's secrets, huh?"

A little embarrassed, I said, "Yes Sir." Then I went back to the galley where my evaluator was waiting.

The first thing he said was, "What did you do wrong?"

I smiled, and said, "Nothing. The General likes my burger."

To Jeff Elder, Many thanks,

His eyebrows rose, slightly; and that was that.

The Chairman then sent his aide back to inquire what was in the burgers. At that point, chef secrets were totally out the window. I admitted to myself that if the General wanted my recipe that bad, I was going to give it to him, and that I did. Later in the flight the Chairman called me up and asked me to sit down and tell him about myself.

As important a man as Chairman Powell was, he made me feel extremely comfortable. We had a great conversation, and that made all the difference in this flight, not to mention my outstanding check ride. When we landed in California, the Chairman thanked me for the burger recipe and mentioned that it was his pleasure to get to know me. The pleasure, I told him, was all mine. No truer words had I ever spoken.

On the dead head home, my evaluator didn't have too many questions as he explained that he was impressed with my behavior in dealing with the Chairman and felt that I was ready for missions alone on the C-20B. I passed my check ride and looked forward to the worldwide missions that were coming my way. I remembered the old adage be careful what you ask for.

—

I received another surprise in March 1989, when I learned I had a second mission to Alaska. This would be my very first mission as a fully qualified. C-20B IPSS was a max load, twelve passengers and an additional pilot which meant six crew members for a total of 18 people on that small aircraft. I was responsible for caring for them all. We set out for a weeklong mission to Alaska, with the Secretary of Interior Manuel Lujan, Jr. and his staff. We were going to view and access the damage caused by the Exxon Valdez Oil Spill in Prince William Sound.

On March 24, 1989, the oil tanker Exxon Valdez struck a reef, tearing open the hull and releasing 11 million gallons of crude oil into the environment. The company's initial response was slow, and a storm blew in, spreading the oil widely. Eventually, more than 1,000 miles of coastline were fouled, and hundreds of thousands of animals perished. At the time, this was the largest oil spill disaster in U.S. history. This week-long trip tested my IPSS skills. Thankfully, all went well and I was surely confident that I could handle this aircraft traveling worldwide alone.

Another C-20B mission was led by Secretary of Defense Dick Chaney. We landed at Twenty-Nine Palms California. We were dropping him off there and deadheading to another location. The

Marines were doing maneuvers in their aircrafts and the Secretary of Defense said to our pilot, "Show them what the Air Force can do when you take off." What did he say that for? Lt. Col. Zappalo was on his "finny flight," and loved the idea. We had to ensure that all things were battened down; he then went to the end of the runway, revved up those Rolls Royce Engines and started down the runway. We had barely got off the runway when I heard the gear doors close, and it was as if we were going straight up like a rocket. I had no idea that the C-20B could do anything like that at all. But I loved every minute of it. It was a nice way for Lt. Col. Zappalo to go out also.

—

I was walking in the Main Exchange at Andrews one day when I noticed someone walking my way, and without thinking, I respectfully greeted him. I saw that it was a general, but I didn't see his name until we were quite close to each other. It was Major General Musser. Without much forethought, I asked him if he had been in Egypt in 1983 during exercises Prized Falcon and Bright Star. The General smiled, and said he was. I immediately introduced myself as one of the airmen who fought the fire at the El Salam Hyatt Hotel. We chatted for a while, and I shared that we had never received the award he suggested for our heroism. The Major General immediately remembered the incident and asked me if I was willing to come by his office and provide him with the details of the fire and the names of the men involved. He gave me his information and location in Cameron Station, Virginia. He also gave me his secretary's contact information. I immediately followed up and set up an appointment for a visit.

I still had a copy of my orders for the exercise that listed all that was involved, and when I presented them to the General, he ensured me this time the award would be processed. In no time at all, I received a message from General Musser. It was great, but not exactly what I expected, saying because the decoration was out of the system for so long, it must be reprocessed as an Accommodation Medal. This was a mild disappointment. The medal would have been a huge help with my promotion, which I missed by just .20 percentage. The air medal would have given me five promotion points. I was happy to receive the Accommodation Medal, and notified all my comrades about the medal. They were all excited and appreciative of my persistence in the matter.

When my Wing Commander presented me with my medal at Commanders Call, he insisted that everyone pay close attention to the citation because this was a very special act of heroism. After the citation was read, my colleagues congratulated me and asked about the experience. To my great surprise, we received three promotion points for the Accommodation Medal. On the next promotion cycle, I was promoted to Staff Sergeant. I can never thank General Musser enough.

Part Five

Expanding the Military Family

Munchie Bear Arrives

Dianna and I had been married almost five years when my first child came along. I guess it was about time. Most parents remember the birth of their children and most definitely their first born. As my wife's due date was nearing, my commander wanted to keep me close to the yard to be there for the birth. On the morning of April 11, 1990, I was scheduled to attend training at the 89th Aircrew Training Center. Prior to my leaving the house that morning, Dianna said she'd experienced some small leakage and was going to her doctor and get checked out just to be safe. Once she got there, the doctor realized it was, in fact, amniotic fluid and admitted her to the Andrews AFB hospital.

The doctor's office contacted my squadron, who then contacted the Learning Center to pass on the message to me. The Learning Center attendant was extremely excited when she told me, "Your wife is about to have that baby and you need to get over to the hospital right away!" While everyone was congratulating me, I was becoming stressed, and focused on getting to the hospital. Once I arrived, I was told it wasn't as much of an emergency as they'd thought, and in fact, the delivery might take a while.

When Dianna was admitted to the hospital at 11 a.m., the doctor learned that her fluid sac had ruptured. Later that evening, he decided to induce labor. They began that process around 6 p.m., and within minutes my wife was feeling true contractions and was squeezing the heck out of my hand. Members of the Oxon Hill congregation had been notified and were there at the hospital in support. Around 8:30 p.m., we saw a baby's head coming out. The first thing I said was, "Yes! No red hair." Finally, at 8:32 pm, with a final push, Dr. Sharp said Mr. & Mrs. Elder, you have a baby girl. I was surprised, since I'd been quite confident I was having a boy. It only took me seconds to get over that. The excitement hit me, and

I said, "I have a girl, I have a girl, we have a girl!"

Dr. Sharp gave me the honor of cutting the umbilical cord. It was such a joy to spend those very first moments of life with my first-born child. The staff then rushed me out of the room as Dianna was having a few complications and I got to go out and tell my congregation members of our new baby girl. Ironically, the last name of the doctor who delivered our baby, Dr. Sharp, was also Dianna's mother's maiden name.

When things finally settled down, I was allowed back in the room to a healthy mother and baby. Dianna named our first-born Brianna Nicole Elder. Beautiful! I gave her the nickname of, "My Little Munchie Bear." I still call her Munch to this day.

—

Lucky for me, I was able to locate a skating rink or roller- rink within miles of every base I lived on. Thank goodness, I was able to continue my passion of Boogie Skating. I was so happy to find that Andrews AF Base had one just a mile away.

Dianna and I lived off base for my first year, but we were able to get on-base housing shortly after that year. We were given a three-bedroom, two story Town House that was more than enough space for the two of us.

Fortunate for me, there was a roller-rink less than a mile outside the back gate of Andrews. The first time I went there, I didn't know anyone. I decided I wouldn't show off as I usually did, so I just skated around at my leisure. That is, until a great song came on and I just had to let loose a little. I was into my groove when I looked behind me and noticed a young guy following me, trying to pick up my moves. When the song was over, we started talking. His name was Paul and he just happened to be a champion classical skater and his mother was the manager of the rink.

Paul introduced me to his mom Patsy, and we instantly formed a friendship. I started coming to the rink several times a week when I was not flying. Patsy became insistent that I no longer pay to get in and skate, and that was fine with me. Paul and I became close friends and I started calling him my little brother. My children called Patsy "Gramma Patsy".

It was a Friday night, March 2, 1991, and I was in Ms. Patsy's office during a break in songs. Around 8:45 p.m. we heard what sounded like several gun shots, and then a car speeding off. We immediately ran outside and saw a young man lying on the ground bleeding. My quick assessment told me the young man had been shot and was unconscious. His pulse was weak and fluttering. At one point, the young man stopped breathing and I lost his pulse.

I immediately began Cardiopulmonary Resuscitation (CPR). After three cycles it seemed to be holding the young man. I continued to perform CPR for about twenty minutes until the Emergency Medical Team (EMT) arrived. The young man regained consciousness and the EMT's transported him to a local hospital. I was feeling very good that I may have saved the young man's life. Unfortunately, I would learn later that he had died at the hospital from the gunshot wounds.

A member of the First Helicopter Squadron (1st Helly) on Andrews, was at the rink and witnessed my efforts to save the young man that night. Without knowing me, he recommended to his leadership that I should be put in for an award or medal for heroism.

On July 1, 1991, Colonel Edward M. Bullard the 89th Military Airlift Wing Commander presented me with The Air Force

Commendation Medal (First Oak Leaf Cluster) for outstanding achievement, prompt action and humanitarian regard for his fellow man.

The Chief Inflight Passenger Service Specialist (IPSS), at the time Chief Master Sergeant (CMSgt) Larry Adams, received information about the incident and was quoted as saying, "Sergeant Elder acted without any hesitation or mental reservation. As a result of his outstanding performance and courageousness, Sergeant Elder was commended by Prince Georges County policeman Paul Evans and the emergency medical response team. All of us here at the 99th MAS are very proud of Sergeant Elder's humanitarian performance."

Part Six

Seeing the World through an Airman's Eyes

Flying in the "Sand Box"

August 7, 1990 was the beginning of "Operation Desert Shield." This was President George Herbert Walker Bush's response to Iraq's invasion of Kuwait on August 2. In support of Operation Desert Shield, President Bush authorized a dramatic increase in U.S. troops and resources in the Persian Gulf.

All of a sudden, the 99th ALS was inundated with flights to what we would call, the "Sand Box," Countries throughout the Middle East. All air crew members had to start a series of Anthrax Vaccinations in the event that the Iraqi Dictator would use this Chemical agent. This stirred up a whirlwind of concern for many as we did not know what side effects would come with these vaccinations. However, if you wanted to continue on flying status you took the vaccinations. I took mine and had no problems with after- effects.

The United States Central Command (Centcom) Headquarters, located at Mac Dill AFB in Tampa, FL, became an alert launch staging facility for those of us in the 99th ALS flying on the C-20 aircrafts. I went down to Mac Dill several times to pull alert. This wasn't so bad. We would alternate the days with two crews and the rest of the time we got to enjoy being in Florida.

I did however fly to the Gulf on several missions on the C- 20 aircraft. On one particular mission, our crew flew out on a two-week trip all over Saudi Arabia, Kuwait, Qatar and then on to Israel. The aircraft we flew on was aircraft tail number 60205. Aircraft 205 was the only C-20 that was plain white, not the traditional blue and white. It was what was described as a "plain wrapper." That white C-20 got extremely dirty when we flew into Kuwait. The Iraqi's had set fire to the Oil wells and they were still burning. Thick black smoke was everywhere, and it was a serious health concern.

We flew over Highway 80 which is a six-lane highway between Kuwait and Iraq. Highway 80 had been used by Iraqi armored divisions for the 1990 Invasion of Kuwait. I took pictures of the many vehicles that had been destroyed along the route.

When we arrived in Saudi Arabia, we had to ensure that all alcohol on the aircraft was sealed, because alcohol is banned there. We billeted at many of the new military bases such as King Khalid Military City which was extremely close to the Iraqi border, and quarters were tight for an aircrew of five.

One of the most memorable parts of this trip was the fact that for the first time, I would stay at the palace of a Saudi Prince. The food was endless, and we even got to make free calls back to the United States. Of course, I called my mother to tell her I was staying at the Prince's Palace. She was both happy and concerned about the trip. I reassured her I was doing well. The nights there were unexpected, and extremely uplifting.

One of our last stops was in Israel. When we flew into Israeli airspace without any warning, our C-20 aircraft was intercepted by two Israeli F-15 Eagles. It was as if they came out of nowhere. We all thanked God that they were friendly.

I had several more flights to the Sand Box. We tried to have at least one flight a month because every time you flew into the War Zone you received Hostile Fire Pay and was Tax Exempt for the month. Those extra dollars came in handy.

—

I always loved flying on the C-20 aircraft. Not only did it have a small passenger load, but it traveled worldwide. There were always some good missions coming up. On one of those particular C-20 missions to Europe, we ran into severe windstorms. While the C-20 is a great plane to fly on, its 77 ft. wingspan causes it to rock in high winds. On this mission, the turbulence was so severe that all of our passengers were getting nervous and scared.

My job as a flight attendant was to make certain passengers are comfortable, and to ensure them we were safe. My seat was a pullout jump seat located in the rear of the aircraft in the middle of the galley. When I was seated, I had full view of all the passengers. During this trip, I noticed most of them were nervous, and when the aircraft did a sudden dip during turbulence, I raised my hands and said, "Folks, this is better than a rollercoaster!" I think it did divert their attention and calm their fears for a while. When the flight normalized, the DV came back and thanked me for putting all of them at ease during such a tense moment. I told him that was just part of the job, and I enjoyed doing it. After the flight, the DV sent a very nice Letter of Appreciation to my Squadron Commander, thanking me for my outstanding service.

Two Weeks on the African Continent

There was always a lot of business for an instructor on the C-20 aircraft. A mission came up that would involve several different countries throughout Africa. We were told this would be a difficult mission because we had to go self- contained. That meant everything that we served on the plane had to be brought with us.

A young man by the name of Kevin Olley was my student on this flight. Kevin and I had traveled a lot on both the C-9 and the C-20 and were very good friends. Once Kevin and I made contact with our onboard representatives, we set out to do our shopping for the mission. When we finished, we had to go and prep as much as we could, then decide how we would store everything.

We had a pretty good plan and now we were going to see how it worked. As is always the case, we got to the plane early. The flight attendants always get to the aircraft before the crew and passengers. When we were getting ready to load, Kevin said, "Jeff, all of this stuff is never going to fit." I promised him it would and asked him to help me get it done. The C-20 is not a huge aircraft, but it has some nice little hiding places. When we were finished, Kevin stood in amazement. I then told him, "I hope you got that, because from hence forth, you are going to be loading it."

On this mission we went to several countries I'd only heard about, and one I'd never heard about –Gulu, Uganda. The airstrip was so small we had to do a fly over to ensure that no livestock was on it before we could land. We were traveling with a Congressional Delegation who were actually going to spend the night in the village huts.

As for the crew, we got to stay in the hotel in town, though it was not your average hotel. We each got our own rooms, but if we wanted hot water, we had to order it the night before. I ordered my hot water and a wakeup call for the next morning. The next morning, I could hear people walking around and then heard a knock on my door. It was one of our crew members, asking me if I was going with them. I asked what time it was, and he said it was crew showtime. I asked him to leave without me, and have the driver return and pick me up. I rushed to get dressed and by the time I was ready the driver was back to get me.

When I got to the aircraft, I explained I hadn't received my requested wakeup call. At that point Kevin said, "I got a wakeup knock on my door, and a bucket of hot water to clean up with." Then he looked at me and said, "Oh, I think that was meant for you, Jeff." We all laughed and were ready to get out of there. When our passengers arrived, they were even more ready to go than we were.

We next went to Kampala, Uganda and landed at the Entebbe Airport which still bore some of the bullet markings from the Raid on Entebbe. We got to stay in a real hotel there and were back to enjoying the comforts of life.

Another highlight of this trip was our trip to Djibouti. I think more than anything I loved the sound of the name. Then we were off to Nairobi, Kenya where Kevin and I were sitting on a balcony hammock eating Klondike Ice Cream sandwiches since we were out of dry ice. We also had the opportunity to dine at the world-famous Carnivore Restaurant. The Carnivore's featured an all-you-can-eat meat buffet. They served a wide variety of meats and were famous for their game like crocodile and Gazelle. At first, I was hesitant, but then I gave in. This was a totally different experience, and we enjoyed ourselves.

Our last adventure of this trip was in Mogadishu, Somalia. We had a lot of trash that we needed to get off the aircraft. One of the guys told us that we could use his Hummer to take the trash to a dump area. Kevin, having served in the Army before, said he knew how to drive a Hummer. There we were, dressed in our suits, driving around in a military dressed out hummer looking for a trash dump area. Again, we took pictures because no one would believe it. This mission turned out to be an excellent training mission for Kevin as he was preparing to fly the C-20 on his own. We also have memories that will last us a lifetime.

The Philippines

In May of 1990, a C-20 mission was generated, and the crew had to be prepared to leave rather quickly. This wasn't an alert launch because we had a day to prepare for it. We were on our way to the Philippines with Richard Armitage, the U.S. special negotiator for the Philippine base negotiations.

I had heard so many stories of life there, and because I had never been to the Philippines, I was looking forward to it. Because of the long crew duty day we would have, we had an additional pilot on the crew. We flew from Andrews to Travis AFB in California, only the beginning of an extremely long day. This stop was great for me because I got to see my Uncle Son, who was a Chief Master Sergeant at Travis. He came out and met the crew on our two-hour ground stop.

From Travis we flew to Hawaii—a refueling stop. I couldn't believe we were in Hawaii, with no ground stop planned, but we were and refueled at Midway Islands. From Midway Island, we flew to Wake Island, and from there to Guam. Finally into Clark Air Base in the Philippines.

When we arrived at Clark AB, the crew had had such a long crew duty day. Over 24 hours. We all agreed to wait until the next day to see the sights of the Philippines. We needed every hour of rest that night. We checked into billeting and I was out for the count. When I woke up the next day and turned on my television, there were news flashes. All personnel were restricted to base and those that were off base were to report back to base.

While we'd been sleeping, two airmen had been killed right after we landed at Clark AB. Philippine Rebels who took responsibility for the killings reported that, "more will be killed until all U.S.

bases, and American occupation soldiers are kicked out of our country."

I was more than angry about the murders, but also very upset that my first time in the Philippines I wouldn't be able to leave the base. As it worked out, I was playing racquetball on base and saw a friend, Aubrey, who I knew from Homestead. It just so happened that he lived off base, there in the Philippines. I was permitted to visit him at his home, and we got to catch up and I got to meet his family. They prepared some excellent Pilipino food. Unfortunately, a year later Mount Pinatubo erupted, virtually destroying Clark AD and many other surrounding areas.

Desert Storm: 1st Alert Launch

Things started heating up in the Middle East. I was watching the news when Operation Desert Storm kicked off. A reporter was broadcasting from the Tel Aviv Hilton and I told my wife, "That's where we stay when we travel to Israel." Now that I was fully qualified on both aircrafts and had my security clearance, I could now pull alert duty. That meant I would have to be available for airborne travel to anywhere in the world, within a 90-minute notification.

Sometime in the middle of the night my beeper went off and I received a phone call from the Andrews AFB Command Post which said I was being alert launched and would receive the details once I reported to the aircraft. I was to go on alert at 0500 for the next two days.

I already had my five-day bag packed. Just had to get dressed and head to the aircraft. Once we all got to the Squadron, we received a briefing and were told where we were going for an undetermined time. We could not pass on this information to any of our loved ones. At that point we were all issued gas masks for the mission. We were heading to Israel. That would be a long flight, stopping a few times to refuel. Our DV was the Deputy Secretary of State Lawrence S. Eagleburger, and the purpose of the trip was an attempt to reassure Israel Prime Minister Yitzhak Shamir's government that it could count on continued U.S. support and to plead for continued Israeli restraint in the gulf conflict.

When we finally arrived in the country, the entire crew was issued another gas mask as were all the residents of Israel. This time our crew was staying at the Dan Hotel which was very close to the U.S. Embassy in Tel Aviv. Not long after we were settled into our rooms, I began doing sit-ups on the floor. An Air Raid alarm went off. I had no clue what is was, but jumped up, thinking it might be a hotel fire alarm. I was near the window and heard the siren whaling outside. At that point I knew this was an Air Raid. I ran to my door and saw all the hotel occupants running to shelter, just as we were briefed on when we arrived.

I started for the shelter, but then, remembered my gas mask was still in my room. I went back to retrieve it. I remember the look of terror on the faces of the people running for safety. I was as terrified as they all were. When I got to the shelter, I saw my other crew members and we waited there watching CNN with Bernard Shaw and Wolf Blitzer. They were giving us information on the SCUD attacks. They also told us when it was all clear and the air raid was over. It is a mixed blessing that most Americans have no idea how it feels to be under attack, or the sound of an air raid alarm.

When the "all clear" was given and I returned to my hotel room, I received a call from the Andrews Command Post. They informed us that they'd reached out to our families and let them know that none of us were injured in the scud attack. I remembered, then, that I hadn't told my family where we were, but now they would know. I knew I had to give them a call right away and reassure them that everything was alright. I was putting on a brave front while talking to my wife trying to keep her calm. Truthfully, if another air raid had gone off while I was on the phone, I would end the call that second, and would be on my way to the shelter again.

This time in Israel was very different. Many of the Holy Land areas were off limits due to violence and threats so we pretty much stayed close to the hotel. After eight days we were leaving. Another long duty day was ahead of us to get back to Andrews. One of our fuel stops was in the Azores.

Right before we landed there, we got word that there was another Scud attack in Israel. For a while we were not sure if we would have to return to Israel. While on the ground at Lages I saw a C-141 Military Transport Aircraft, which was heading to Andrews. I recall thinking to myself: This is the plane that I need to be on. But after a little while, we were given clearance to proceed to Andrews. The whole crew breathed a sigh of relief.

Finally, after a very long crew duty day, we landed at Andrews. Normally after landing, the flight attendant has another hour to an hour and half of cleaning up the aircraft ensuring that it is mission ready. It must have been my lucky day because I was met by a cleanup crew and they let me gather my belongings and go straight home. Boy, did I need that.

Sally

All the flying I was doing helped me save money. We got per diem for every trip, and as a flight attendant we had access to all the food. I thought I needed to make myself an investment, so I found a vintage 1966 Mustang Convertible down in southern Maryland. It was midnight blue with a white rag top and two tone aqua blue interior. Kevin Olley, being mechanically inclined drove down with me and inspected the car. I immediately fell in love with her, and when Kevin gave his ok, I bought her on the spot. I named her Sally. Kevin drove my other car back to Andrews.

My love affair with Sally began the day I purchased her and has never waned. My daughters loved riding with the top down as I jokingly pretended that my hair was blowing in the wind. On one occasion my great niece and nephew visited from Niagara Falls. They were six and seven at the time, and I took them and my two girls for a ride to Historic Old Towne in Alexandria, Virginia. As we came to a stop light on King Street, the song "Hip Hop Hurray," came on.

So, I started waving my hands back and forth like in the song, then my daughters joined in as we all kept singing. Eventually, my young niece and nephew joined in.

Suddenly, we noticed that some of the people along the street started doing the hip-hop hurray wave and my nephew looked at me and said, "Wow! Uncle Jeffrey. That was a classic moment, just like something from the movie *Ferris Buller's Day Off*.

Volon Spouse Flights

The Volon Spouse was an event the flying squadrons at Andrews tried to schedule at least once each year, but I can remember it occurring only three times while I was at Andrews. During Volon Spouse, Air Force members' spouses were treated to a flight over Niagara Falls. They would also be treated to a special meal prepared by the flight attendants, with each given a beautiful rose. Basically, it was our opportunity to spoil our spouses.

Normally, a crew member would not get to fly on the same aircraft that their spouse was invited to join. The rules were based on the very real possibility that an aircraft could go down for whatever reason. The Air Force didn't want both spouses to die and leave children parentless. However, in some instances the rules were bent a bit, as was the case for me and a few other crew members.

The flight attendants were responsible for planning the meal, doing all of the shopping, preparing and serving the meals. Each crew position did their part in making these flights a very special occasion for the spouses. This is the same Sam Fox service provided for all Distinguished Visitor's (DV's). Spouses, however, were our DV's for those flights.

This event also gave me another opportunity to brag about my hometown of Niagara Falls as we were circling over the Falls. Needless to say, everybody knew where I was from, and that I was extremely proud of it.

Flying Dignitaries to Niagara Falls

Being from Niagara Falls, when any missions came up going there, the flight attendant scheduler usually put me on that mission. When the dignitaries found out I was from Niagara Falls, it presented me with an opportunity to brag about the city that I loved so well. I would often get asked where they should go and what should they do while they were there. I was always ready with an answer.

Niagara Falls, NY had so many attractions and depending on the time of the year dictated my response. Of course, Niagara Falls, Ontario had many more attractions, but I would tell everyone that most people go to Niagara Falls, Ontario to see the beauty of the American side. That was my story, and I was sticking to it.

There was the Winter Garden, Festival of Lights and ice skating in front of the old Convention Center in the winter, and during the summer months who could pass up a trip through the Cave of the Winds or a ride on the Maid of the Mist right up to the base of the Falls. No matter what time of year, Niagara Falls, NY always had a lot to offer.

Anytime we flew foreign dignitaries to Niagara Falls, the State Department was the sponsor for the mission. That meant that all funds came from them and our menus were approved through them. That also meant that Mr. Payne was going to be there taking care of all the passengers' baggage.

Mr. Payne was always dressed as if he was heading to the finest dinner. As an IPSS, I too, took personal pride in presenting a great image to the public. On several occasions when we had trips to Niagara Falls, my mother would come out to the plane and when Mr. Payne would see my mom, he would tell her that I was the sharpest dressed man on Andrews. Of course, my mom would always agree.

—

It was an exciting day when I graduated to flying on Air Force Two (AF-2). What most civilians don't know, is that AF-2 is not one specific aircraft, but any aircraft transporting the Vice President of the United States. The Vice President at the time was George H. W. Bush, and we had an out and back mission to New York City. The crew stayed on the aircraft while the Vice President attended his meetings. When he arrived back at the airplane, the crew prepared for takeoff back to Andrews.

Prior to taking the runway, the pilot stopped and came in to discuss a matter with the Vice President and his advisers.

He then proceeded to the rear of the aircraft to brief the rest of the crew that there had been a missile threat to us after we took off. We were to ensure that everything was locked up and strapped in as we would do a Max performance take off.

Our Aircraft Commander, Lt. Colonel Jessie Glisson was around five feet tall and weighed a little over 100 pounds. But this man could fly the heck out of that VC-9C. I was sitting on the rear jump seat door and heard the engines revved up to max. When the pilot released the brakes, the aircraft darted down the runway like I'd never experienced before. Once we were airborne, we climbed to 10,000 feet in no time at all. At that point we would have been out of any danger and we all breathed a sigh of relief.

—

Being a member of the Air Force One crew was one of the highlights of my military career. I was a flight attendant in the 99th Airlift Squadron and I had made it to the top of what we call the food chain. I was an Evaluator. As an evaluator we could pretty much go on the missions we chose to go on. But it could also be a lot of work, as you always had to be the example and set the benchmark for new flight attendants.

I had been at Andrews for several years and was not looking to move to any other duty assignments. One day I came in and the flight attendant scheduler told me that somebody from the Air Force Military Personnel Center (AFMPC), also known as Assignments, had called from San Antonio, Texas. I wondered out loud, why were they looking for me? In fact, one of the pilots stationed at Andrews, went to our sister squadron in Belgium and mentioned my name as a possible IPSS replacement.

As I was talking to the flight attendant scheduler, the person from Assignments called again. The scheduler said, "Yes, here he is."

When I answered the phone, the person asked if I was interested in an Assignment at Chievres Air Base in Belgium. I replied, "I am totally not interested."

The person then told me that I had been requested and that I didn't have to go right then, but I'd be due soon for reassignment.

The wheels started turning in my brain. I knew the Presidential Pilots Office (PPO) was looking to hire new people, and I was definitely ready to pursue other options. But the first time they wanted me to fly with them, I was at the National Racquetball Championships in Houston, Texas. As soon as I returned, they scheduled flights for me. One of the first crew members to greet me was Joe Efferd, a flight engineer from the AF-1 crew. I asked Joe, "What would I need to do to become a member of the AF-1 crew?"

Joe said, "Jeff, just be yourself." I laughed and told him nobody could be me better than me.

Work in PPO was totally different from what I was doing at the 99th. I was a worker bee starting at the bottom of the food chain. This was fine because I loved flying on that big beautiful plane, and a lot of flying they did; which kept us extremely busy. We even had a dress code for our ground stops which consisted of what we called "PPO Pants," either slacks or khakis. No jeans, which was great for me because I didn't own a pair of jeans. Everybody thought it was weird that I didn't wear jeans, but I had been that way for a long time and wasn't planning to change.

As it turned out, my good friend and fellow 99th ALS flight attendant, D. Lynwood Crenshaw, volunteered for the assignment in Belgium and that gave me more time. I was really enjoying flying with the Presidential Organization. Colonel Barr was the Presidential Pilot at the time. He was a much-respected man who had more power than a lot of Generals in the Air Force. He used this power to take care of his people in the AF-1 organization.

The PPO flight attendants would have a vendor appreciation party every year around Christmas to thank those vendors who supplied and supported them throughout the year. We were all standing around in the flight attendant break room when Col. Barr came in. As he started thanking the vendors for their support he then said, "We don't usually do this, but I just wanted to take a moment and ask Jeff Elder if he would like to become a permanent member of the Air Force One Crew."

I was in shock, and stood there speechless, for a moment. The Colonel was looking at me, waiting for an answer, so I gathered myself and finally said, "Yes Sir, I do."

Colonel Barr shook my hand and said, "Welcome, Jeff, to the AF-1 Family."

Everyone began applauding and congratulating me on my promotion. I made it. With that, I didn't have to worry about that Belgium assignment or any other assignment as I would now be coded to stay on Andrews.

Getting hired on AF-1 was extremely hard to do, and it was just as easy to get fired if you did not fit the mold. It was like a written rule that you would never discuss religion, politics or, bottom line, anything that could be construed as controversial. Another thing was, it did not matter whether you were a Democrat, Republican or Independent. You served honorably no matter who was in office. So, when the Presidents changed, the crew would say goodbye to the old administration and hello to the new business as usual.

—

Once you get hired on AF-1, crew members that have been there for a while always ask one question. "You got a Hawk?"

That was their way of letting you know that you were still brand new to the AF-1 family. The Hawk is slang for the Presidential Service Badge (PSB). The PSB is a badge awarded to members of the military that serve as full-time staff to the President of the United States of America. You had to be on assignment for 12 months before you could even apply for a PSB.

Once I finally received my PSB, the question became, "What's the number of your Hawk?"

I would proudly respond: "The number of my Hawk or PSB is 15382. Behind that number at the National Archives is the name Jeffrey Elder."

We were presented with our PSB, at a formal ceremony conducted by the AF-1 Commander. I was extremely excited when it was my turn to receive my PSB. Colonel Barr was officiating and when he pinned my PSB on me, everybody started laughing. I had no clue as to what was going on. Then I looked down and noticed that there was a picture of a chicken wing taped over my PSB. That is why everybody was laughing. I got a good chuckle out of it also. Colonel Barr then presented me with my real PSB.

Colonel Barr was large and in charge but at the same time, he was a very down to earth man. I think he was the last AF-1 Commander who had total control of the Air Force One organization. Colonel Barr, thank you for allowing me to be a part of the AF-1 family.

Leaving Andrews AF Base

After living in Base Housing for eight years, the time had come for our housing unit to be renovated. I was given the option of moving to another location on base or the government would pay for my move off base. Well, that was a no brainer. My wife and I started looking for a home off base.

I mentioned this to one of my good friends, Robin Duble, who I played racquetball with and he told me that he now owned his own mortgage company and that he would love to assist us with prequalifying and getting a home loan. Although I had heard horror stories about people trying to get their first mortgage loan, I trusted Robin. All I did was give him our financial information and proof of employment and he did the rest.

In no time at all we were prequalified.

Now we just had to find a home that we wanted to buy. That was the painful process. We looked and looked. When I was traveling, I would give Dianna a list of potential homes to look at. On one particular trip to the West Coast, I had given her a list, and Dianna called me up sounding like she was out of breath. I immediately thought something was wrong.

Dianna said, "I found our home." She went on to say, it has four bedrooms upstairs and three and a half baths. It also had an In-Law apartment in the basement.

But there was a problem. The owner wanted to get out of the place ASAP. That meant he was looking to close in record time. I was scheduled to get back to Andrews Friday morning. He had two other offers on Wednesday and wanted Dianna to make him an offer. I told her that if she felt that strongly about it to go ahead and make an offer. Dianna thought about it and then consulted her father, Darryl. He told her she should probably wait for Jeff to see it before making an offer and she agreed.

Our Real Estate Agent, Frank was very good at what he does. He told the homeowner that I was away on travel with the President and I'd be back on Friday morning. At that time, I would come and view the house and make an offer and at that point he can look at all three offers at the same time. The homeowner reluctantly agreed. When we landed, my chief allowed me to leave right away to view the house. When I saw the home the first thing that I thought was: *Ok, what is wrong with this house that he wants to get out of it so quick?*

The homeowner then explained that he was going through a divorce and he needed to liquidate right away. At that point we made him an offer. Our offer was significantly smaller than the other two offers, but we were prequalified and had money ready to start the process. The homeowner rejected our offer and asked our agent for us to raise it.

Hey, I was a Staff Sergeant in the United States Air Force. The amount that we offered was practically out of reach for us any way. There was no way that we were going to offer more. Two days went by and the homeowner called my agent and asked if we were able to offer more. When my agent said no, he accepted our offer and wanted to proceed right away.

The price we got our home for meant that we went into it with instant equity. We felt like the Jeffersons. We were moving on up. What a difference being prequalified made. I thank Robin, for all of his assistance.

When it came time for the closing, I was scheduled to be out of town on another mission. No surprise. We had to get a power of attorney and Dianna had to not only sign all those papers with her name, but also for me. All things worked out and we were set to move in to our first home the end of November 1996. I wanted a place for my daughters to call home that was for them. This was it.

Thank God, I got promoted to Technical Sergeant not long after that. So, in July of 1997, we planned a housewarming and Promotion party. We planned it for the 4th of July. Don't you know an AF-1 mission came up, leaving on the night of the 4th? Because I had already made such extensive plans, they allowed me to miss the AF-1 mission and I would then take the First Lady mission leaving on the following Monday.

I loved flying the First Lady missions overseas. There was always great shopping, and the prices didn't go up as they did when the POTUS traveled to a site. The First Lady mission was going to be for 20 days. We were to meet up with the AF-1 crew in Madrid Spain for five nights, and then the President and First Lady would go separate ways. After Spain, the FLOTUS mission went to two different locations in Austria then five nights in Portugal before coming back to Andrews. This was to be Chelsea Clinton's last trip before going off to college.

Presidential Pushups

We were on an AF-1 mission and I walked into the Guest Compartment where Rebecca, one of the flight attendants, was having a conversation with President Clinton about physical fitness. When I walked up, Rebecca told President Clinton I was a fitness buff, and used to do a lot of sit-ups and pushups. The President looked over and asked if there was anything special about the way I did my pushups. I tried to explain, but it was much easier for me to show him.

So, in my suit I got down on the floor and did some pushups. President Clinton observed, then said, "Let me try some of them." He then got down on the floor and popped out a few of the pushups in the same manner as I. When he stood back up, he said he really did feel the difference.

We talked a little longer about physical fitness before the President went back to the front of the aircraft. A short while later, Ralph one of the Official Photographers came back with his head down. I said, "Ralph, you missed me and the President doing pushups on AF-1." Ralph apologized and told me he would make it up to me. I said, "No problem." He had already provided me with some outstanding pictures.

A Presidential Stop in Buffalo

A few weeks later, we had an AF-1 mission going to Buffalo, just 16 miles from Niagara Falls, my hometown. Any time a mission was going to or near our hometown, we were usually placed on that mission and sometimes were given the special perk of having the President meet our family and friends.

Mike Evans and I were from the Buffalo area and we both had our families coming out for the event. This mission was going to be on two VC-9C aircrafts. There were two photographers on the mission, and Ralph was one of them. He assured me that he would get some good photos of me and my family with the President, and he didn't let me down.

This event was huge and there were people everywhere. One of the President's aides asked me if my family was in place. I told them they were out in the crowd, and up to that point I couldn't locate them. He told me to get up on the edge of the stage and see if I could locate them. Once I got up there, I was able to see my 6' 5" brother-in-law and directed my family to the rally point.

When the President finished addressing the crowd, he turned his attention to first, Mike's family, then mine. The President first met my mother and father and the first thing he said to them is that I take great care of him and that I am his personal fitness trainer on Air Force One. When he said that my mouth was wide open and of course Ralph was snapping pictures. He told my parents they had done a wonderful job in raising me and talked me up so much, that I felt like the most important person around. It was a very special moment that we will never forget.

The President then said, "Jeff let's take a picture with just me you and your mom and dad first."

Following that, he took an individual picture with every person in my family group. Lastly, he took a picture with the entire group. My mother grabbed the President and I immediately said, "Mom, you can't grab the President like that."

President Clinton with Jeff and His Parents, in Buffalo

But the President looked at me and said, "Jeff, you know I love this." And he grabbed my mother back. I looked over at Lew Merletti, the head Secret Service Agent, and he gave me an "it's okay" look. I was relieved.

—

Mike Evans introduced me to his friend Lorraine Goszewski, who owned the Heritage Inn in West Seneca, NY. Over time, we all became very good friends. Anytime either the President or First Lady had a mission to Niagara Falls or Buffalo, we could count on Lorraine and her family to provide us with the finest local cuisine of Buffalo wings, pizza and hot Beef on weck sandwiches, just to name a few.

On this mission, Lorraine invited the entire AF-1 crew, Mike and my family members and even our advance agents to a special dinner at the Heritage Inn. When we arrived, we all walked in together and everybody in the restaurant stopped, stood up and started applauding all of us. The piano player was playing the Air Force Song *Off We Go into the Wild Blue Yonder*. Everyone wanted to come up and greet us, shake our hands and thank us for our service. This was an outstanding evening and I am so thankful that my family could be a part of it. Lorraine and her entire family had the biggest hearts and we could not thank them enough for making all of us feel like true heroes. Unfortunately, the historic Heritage Inn was lost to a devastating fire in 2004. Thank God nobody was hurt. Thank you, Lorraine and the Goszewski family for everything. You are true heroes.

Weeks after our Buffalo trip, we were on another AF-1 mission and the President saw me and asked if I had gotten the pictures from the Official Photographer. I said, "Yes." And he asked for them so that he could sign them. I already had a post it on all of them so that he knew who to sign them to. By the end of the flight, I was given my envelope of pictures back and the President had signed every one of them. On my next visit to Niagara Falls, I was able to deliver the signed pictures to my elated family members.

Wind Turbulence on AF-1

President Clinton traveled to New Mexico to wrap up a three-day West Coast campaign trip that included a brief stop in Las Vegas and two nights in California. It was Tuesday, June 12, 1996. While on our ground stop in New Mexico, we catered an authentic Mexican meal for the President which included red chili cheese enchiladas with beans, rice and salsa.

When we departed New Mexico for Charleston, South Carolina, things were normal. By the time we flew over Lubbock, Texas, all hell broke loose. I was walking to the front of the aircraft when the first jolt occurred. Ralph, the photographer was walking down the aisle when he suddenly was thrown up toward the ceiling. When he came down, he was crawling on his knees. I immediately strapped him into an empty seat in the staff compartment. Just in time for the second jolt. At that point, we were both strapped in and holding on for dear life.

When things settled down, I released my seatbelt and started checking on the passengers to ensure that everybody was alright. Thank God, the President was not injured! All 46 passengers and 26 crewmen were good, with the exception of one Secret Service Agent who slightly cut his hand. Turbulence usually hits the rear of the aircraft the hardest and in this case it certainly did.

When I got to the rear galley it looked like a bomb had gone off. Glasses and dishes were smashed, and food was spattered all over the floor, walls and ceiling. Not just any food, but brightly colored Mexican food. I went to find my camera to take photos, because I knew no one would believe it was as bad as it really was. We immediately closed the press room's door to avoid pictures being sent across the airwaves.

Unfortunately, there would be no more food served from the rear galley during the flight. The cleaning began and the forward galley finished serving the rest of the passengers and crew.

Shortly after things settled, President Clinton walked through the plane and told the press how he was sitting reading up front in the plane's oval office when the turbulence hit. The President told the reporters, "It was certainly a character builder, wasn't it?" He laughed, and said, "I was holding on. I was holding on."

When we landed, I was responsible for taking the Limo Kit to the limo. As I was putting the kit into the limo, I felt someone behind me. When I looked back, I saw that it was President Clinton's Secret Service Agent, which meant the President was already on his way to the car. The agent said, "Go ahead Jeff." But I hurried and finished so the President could go. I remember thinking that I'd never seen the President get off the plane that quick before.

One thing our crew had a laugh about later, was that this was the first time Colonel Barr had let Lt. Col. Donnelly, the Deputy AF-1 Pilot, have command of AF-1 by himself. We joked that Col. Barr gave Donnelly the keys to the plane and he almost wrecked it.

The truth was that AF 1 flew near some electrical storms, and that was the cause of the severe turbulence.

President's Florida Injury

The AF 1 crew was scheduled for a several-day trip to Naples, Florida. When we landed it was raining cats and dogs, so we didn't do anything that evening. Good thing we didn't, because early the next morning we were alerted that the President had injured himself, and we and AF-1 would be returning to Andrews.

Little did we know, it was going to be a great ordeal just getting the President onboard AF-1. Several crew members were tasked with helping lift the President up the stairs in a lightweight evacuation chair. To my knowledge, this was something that had not been practiced before.

President Clinton was at the residence of Greg Norman when his injury occurred and when he returned to the aircraft, Mr. Norman and his wife accompanied him. As it turned out, Mr. Norman's wife was a former Flight Attendant. So, while the President was being loaded onto the aircraft, The Normans came up to meet our flight attendants. We all conversed for a while and Mr. Norman provided us with some signed photographs of himself.

Once we arrived back at Andrews, it was easier getting the President from the aircraft. We used our catering vehicle to lower the President which alleviated our having to navigate the stairs. The First Lady met AF-1 to accompany the President to the hospital. All crew members on that mission received the Air Force Achievement Medal for aiding in the quick turnaround return flight to Andrews Air Force Base after the President's injury.

The Longest Day

One of my longest crew duty days was on President Clinton's Middle East Tour in which he visited Egypt, Jordan, Syria, Israel, Kuwait and Saudi Arabia. It was well into the trip and we started the morning in Tel Aviv, Israel after our long night of "experiencing the culture." We had a crew show time of 0700 which would allow us to get to the aircraft two hours prior to takeoff.

Our first flight was to Kuwait City for a five-hour ground stop then off to Saudi Arabia. As we were preparing for landing, I took my seat at door 5L and my crew mate Rob was at 5R. We experienced a very rough landing and as I looked out the window at 5L, I noticed a lot of black smoke and rubber flying by. I looked over at Rob and we didn't know if we were on fire or what. Hearing no commands from the pilot we thought that we were all right.

Once we were able to come to a full stop and the passengers deplaned, I was able to go outside to check out what had happened. Upon landing, the aircraft blew five tires. Yes, five. Each 747 always carried two spare tires, which meant another tire had to be flown in from a different location. 747 tires are huge and weigh a lot. The good thing is that this was the Backup 747, so it would not delay the President at all.

After our scheduled ground time, AF-1 took off for its 14.5- hour flight back to Andrews. It would be some time before the fifth tire would even show up and then, it would still have to be changed. Finally, all the tires were changed, and the backup aircraft was ready to take off for our flight back to Andrews. That was a very long crew duty day.

President Clinton's Africa Trip

One of the greatest experiences of my life was witnessing, firsthand, how President Clinton was received on his first trip to Africa in 1998. The crew set out on a six-country, 12- day mission to Ghana, Rwanda, Kampala Summit, South Africa, Botswana, and Senegal. For AF-1, 12 days on the road is a long trip.

It started when we landed. All engines went silent and even the Auxiliary Power Units that ran the aircraft air conditioning was turned off. The welcoming ceremony was most impressive. The African people were dressed in traditional garb and when they started dancing, I had to pinch myself as I was seeing something that I had only seen on television. It was truly remarkable.

Another thing that I was impressed with was the great numbers of people of color everywhere you looked. It was like I saw so many people that looked like somebody that I know in the World. You know they say that we all have a twin somewhere.

Everywhere we went there were massive crowds gathering to greet the American President. As we drove to our hotel, thousands lined the route waving American flags. We all felt like rock stars.

President Bush's Top-Secret Trip to Iraq

During President George W. Bush's presidency, the AF-1 crew spent nearly all Holidays in Texas and the whole month of August, there. Did I happen to mention that August is extremely hot in Texas? Moreover, not just anywhere in Texas but Waco, Texas. The President's Ranch was not far away in Crawford, Texas.

President Bush Congratulates Jeff on His Promotion to Master Sergeant

The President would always make sure the AF 1 crew was taken care of and not just sitting around doing nothing on holidays. One of those holidays just happened to be Thanksgiving Day. Another perk of traveling with the President on holidays was that we always managed to get outstanding tickets to the Dallas Cowboys vs. Washington Redskins football game.

Here was my dilemma: spend some wonderful time with people that considered me family or hang out at a football game, when I wasn't crazy about either of the teams. The choice was obvious. My best friend Richard Eisemann always invited me to his home, which was right outside Dallas, to eat Thanksgiving dinner with him and his family. Richard was also my racquetball doubles partner. The highlight for me, of course, was that I got to carve the family turkey. I always thoroughly enjoyed myself with the Eisemann family, and it had become something of a tradition that we all looked forward to each year.

Of course, the plan in 2003, was to do the same thing on Thanksgiving Day. At least, that had been the plan. On Wednesday evening, AF-1 Commander, Colonel Mark Tillman told us we'd be taking the Aircraft back to Andrews to take care of some maintenance issues. I immediately reached out to Ice as I called him and let him know I would probably be late for dinner and they might have to start without me.

When the crew reported to the aircraft for our supposed flight back to Andrews, Colonel Tillman had us all go to the conference room for a crew brief. He started our brief with, "At this point, I want everybody to turn off their cell phone and there will be absolutely no communication with anybody in the world." After we all followed his instructions, he said, "We are on our way to Iraq." For some of the newer crewmembers who had no idea something like this could happen, they were in awe, their mouths wide open. Colonel Tillman explained point by point, what we would be doing during this trip. After he ended his briefing, we all went about our business as normal.

President Bush was unrecognizable when he arrived at the aircraft and came up through the rear stairs. First, he never walked up the rear steps. Second, he was wearing an overcoat with jeans, cowboy boots, a button-down shirt, and a baseball cap. There was also a handful of news and magazine reporters and photographers along for the ride.

Just like that, our backup plane became Air Force One. But, of course, we were not using that call sign. Our flight to Andrews would take nearly three hours. Once we arrived at Andrews, things were so hush, hush that the Base Commander had no clue that we were even there. The Aircraft taxied right up to the AF-1 hangar. The hangar doors opened, and we were towed in.

Once inside, all crew and passengers deplaned and got on the other 747 that was already fueled and supplied with all provisions for the trip. At that point, some other journalist joined our group. All of our press people had to remove their phone batteries and place all communications items in the belly of the aircraft until a time deemed safe.

Shortly after 11p.m. EST: Air Force One departed Andrews for an extremely long flight to Iraq. Onboard were the President, a hand full of his Senior Staff, Secret Service, 13 press and the rest were AF-1 crew.

It was stressed by the White House Communications Director that if there were any leaks of the trip that the aircraft would turn around and abort the mission. Even some of the AF-1 phones were turned off to ensure the secrecy of the mission.

With less than a half hour to touchdown, all the cabin lights were turned off and all window shades were closed. That is when Col Tillman started a cork barrel landing approach into Bagram Air Base, Iraq.

Once we landed, we were instructed that anyone getting off the aircraft had to have a flak jackets on for protection.

Having come all this way, I wanted to experience actual time on the ground in Iraq. I donned a flak jacket and went outside and walked around the aircraft. I didn't spend a lot of time out there, but it was an experience that I will never forget. I wondered how it must feel for those military members stationed there.

We were only on the ground two and a half hours. It was only after AF-1 took off and reached a safe altitude that the news was released that the President of the United States just visited the troops in Iraq for a Thanksgivings Day Dinner.

Can you imagine how surprised and angry those who wanted to harm the President felt when they found out that he was actually there? We made it. The mission was a complete success. President Bush was walking around the aircraft in an extremely exhilarated mood.

Sometime into the flight of an extremely long day, I was on the couch right outside the forward galley catching a cat nap when I opened my eyes to see President Bush right over me. He then leaned back up and gave his very noticeable laugh and walked away. I then looked at another flight attendant Reggie and said, "What just happened?"

He said the President was in a good mood and he was messing with me. I have always wondered what he would have done if I didn't wake up.

Now that the news was released to the world, back in Texas my friend Ice was watching television when the breaking news came in. He turned around and told his family, "Jeff ain't coming."

They all totally understood, but there were many others on the President's ranch and at Andrews who thought they should have been in on the plan.

Colonel Tillman later said a British Airways aircraft saw us and asked if he had just seen AF-1. Colonel Tillman replied on the radio, "No, we're Gulfstream 5."

This was just another close call for aborting the mission.

When we arrived back in Texas on Friday morning, there was excitement, jubilation and a lot of questions. As for the aircrew, most of the flight attendants went out to breakfast at IHOP. We all had been up for an extremely long time with just a cat nap here and there. There was also a sense of accomplishment having been a part of the President's first trip to Iraq and his most unusual Presidential Trip.

President Reagan's Funeral Flight

In June of 2004, President George W. Bush was on a European trip to Rome Italy, Vatican City and several places in France. Many of us flight attendants were out sightseeing in Paris when we came across some of the crew communications operators and they communicated to us that former President Reagan had just passed away.

Hearing that news many of us wondered if our trip would get cut short. As it turned out, the European portion was not.

However, when we left Europe, we were heading straight to Georgia, for the G8 Summit. Once we arrived in Georgia, the AF-1 Backup aircraft headed back to Andrews to prepare to fly out to California to pick up former President Reagan's body and Mrs. Reagan and bring them to Washington, DC so that the President's body could lie in State at the Capitol Rotunda.

This was the first time that the VC747 had been used to travel with a casket. Preparations were made to have the casket in the Guest Compartment. I had the honor of being the number two Pall Bearer when we brought President Reagan's casket onboard the aircraft. Only AF-1 crewmembers were utilized to take the casket both on and off the aircraft.

The flight back to California was extremely solemn. Mrs. Reagan spent nearly the entire flight right next to the casket. Margret Thatcher's aide came to the rear of the airplane and we were talking. I told her that I was a huge fan of Mrs. Thatcher and she insisted that I go up and meet her.

When I went up to the conference room, I saw former Prime Minister Margaret Thatcher. I introduced myself and told her how much of a fan I was. She was very gracious and thanked me. As this was going on, Mr. Merv Griffin who was sitting on the other side of the conference room table said, "Hey, what are we, chopped liver?"

I immediately said to him, "Oh Sir, I will be happy to visit with you, as I used to always watch the Merv Griffin Show."

He smiled and waited for me to finish with Mrs. Thatcher.

I thanked Mr. Griffin for his many years of public service and the many television shows that he brought to us as we shared a photo or two. This was a very uplifting moment for those in the conference room as it made all of us smile, at least for a moment.

U.S. Presidential Campaigns

I have worked five Presidential Campaigns. The first was the 1988 campaign of then Vice President George Herbert Walker Bush. Leading up to Super Tuesday was the beginning of my campaign flying. At that time, crews were going through their crew duty day hours so fast that replacement crews had to be positioned at different locations to keep the crews legal.

On Super Tuesday alone we visited seven different cities. That was seven different takeoffs and landings in one day and for the flight attendant, that was seven different meals. At the end of that day, another crew came in to continue the mission on the next day. Welcome to the world of Air Force Two.

On that Election Day, it just so happened that I was in the middle of Aircrew Survival Training School located at Fairchild AFB in Spokane, Washington. As part of the course curriculum, we underwent physiological training to include sleep denervation, evade and escape, and what to do once captured by an enemy. Being sleep deprived in a POW camp, our instructors told us Michael Dukakis was elected as the next President of the United States. Being kept away from any of the news sources, that is what we thought had happened, right up until we got out of the POW Camp. Oh, our instructors were really good at their jobs.

My second campaign was the 1992 reelection campaign of George H.W. Bush. I was still an AF-2 Flight Attendant, so our time was focused on travel of the Vice President, James Danforth Quayle. Vice President Quayle kept us extremely busy during his four years in Office.

At one particular ground stop, the VP and Mrs. Quayle left their children, Tucker, Benjamin and Corinne, on the plane. I guess the valet was supposed to be looking after them, but that didn't happen. I was down talking to aircraft security when another crew member came down and said, "Those kids are up there running and jumping all over the seats."

Just as I got to the main cabin, I saw Benjamin jumping over one of the seats. I said, "Hey! What's going on? You can't just jump all over the seats like that. You guys need to sit down and act like you got some sense." They immediately calmed down.

When the VP and Mrs. Quayle returned, I was helping the VP take off his jacket and the children came in and told them what happened and what I had said to them. Mrs.

Quayle looked at me, and truthfully, I was sweating bullets, thinking my career was now out the window. Then she looked at her children and said, "Well, somebody needs to keep you guys in line."

We all smiled, but I was breathing a sigh of relief. From that point on, we never had any issues again and the kids were very respectful. I guess they were just trying to see what they could get away with.

The campaign was extremely busy leading right up to election night. For our efforts, the entire crew was invited to the election night celebration, which was held in Indianapolis, IN. Air Force Two Flight Attendants from both the 99th and 1st Airlift Squadrons were the only flight attendants allowed on that flight.

While it was a celebration of sorts, it wasn't long into the evening before most of us knew that it wouldn't be a long- lasting celebration. Arkansas Governor William Jefferson Clinton was leading in the polls and was coming out on top. Most everybody put on a smiling face, but it was really tough for most. This was an outstanding opportunity for the crew as they allowed us to share in this moment.

The Vice President's Office also invited all the Flight Attendants to their last Christmas Social before leaving Office, held at the VP's residence, the U.S. Naval Observatory. This was a wonderful opportunity for me because I was able to bring not only my wife, Dianna, but also my two-year-old daughter Brianna to the event. One of the highlights of this evening was a wonderful picture of my family and the Quayle Family with Marilyn Quayle holding Brianna.

President Clinton Reelection Campaign

The 1996 Clinton Reelection campaign was indeed one of the most grueling for the AF-1 crew. It is a major production anytime this plane takes off, and to take off and land sometimes six times in a day is truly demanding on the crew. But we all volunteered for it and campaigns only come once every four years, so we had to suck it up and press on.

This campaign was very memorable because this was the first time that I experienced the Air Force One Campaign and all of the inner workings. Finally, after months of none stop traveling, came election night. The entire crew was invited to the Arkansas State House where the election night celebration was to be held. It was an extremely festive atmosphere as we all knew that President Clinton would be reelected.

A group of us flight attendants were walking around enjoying the sites when we saw Ann Compton, a White House correspondent for ABC News. She came up to us congratulating and thanking us for taking (in her words) outstanding care of them during this campaign. Mrs.

Compton had always been a pleasure to serve, and she always enjoyed her flight on AF-1. Of course, the partying went well into the night.

2000 Gore Election Campaign

My next campaign was the most different of all. This was when Vice President Gore was the Heir Apparent for the Presidency. Or at least we thought. The Vice President made what many still believe was a fatal mistake of distancing himself from President Clinton and not embracing the Clinton record.

In November of 1998, the Air Force One crew was all set for a mission to Malaysia to attend the APEC Summit. Things in Iraq were heating up and the crew was put on alert that we would leave at a moment's notice for the summit. The entire crew repositioned from Andrews AFB to Dulles Airport in Virginia which had a much longer runway. That way, when we found out the mission was a go, we could have enough fuel onboard to fly direct to Kuala Lumpur.

When the message came in that we would be departing, it also stated that President Clinton would not be making the trip and that Vice President Gore would. Due to the late time, the only aircraft that would get him to the summit on time was the backup AF-1, 747. So, the AF-1 crew on the backup aircraft took off from Dulles as Air Force Two on an extremely long flight to Kuala Lumpur.

When we finally arrived in Kuala Lumpur, we were exhausted and had to get some rest. I have to say that after our rest, our crew partied like it was 1999 as the song goes. This was our first time out on a mission overseas without the Chief AF-1 pilot. Some called it "no adult supervision," or that time the kids got to take the plane out and play. Of course, we did everything we were supposed to, just in a more relaxed environment.

After the summit was over, we took off for Hawaii where we

dropped off the Vice President and another 89thaircraft picked him up to transport him back to Washington, DC. Once we landed back in the U.S (Hawaii), President Clinton departed Washington DC for what was the rest of the original mission in the Pacific to Japan and Korea. The longtime rule in the world of presidencies is that the President and Vice President cannot be out of the Country at the same time.

Our crew was able to spend one night in Hawaii, then we flew to Japan to rejoin the primary aircraft and continue the mission as the AF-1 Backup. We all had an outstanding time being away from the primary and all that prestige.

The crew got a taste of what we thought was to come in a Gore Presidency. The Vice President and his Staff thoroughly enjoyed their time aboard the Presidential aircraft. Many pictures were taken and a whole lot of phone calls made. The crew was literally worn out.

Unfortunately, that was the only time Mr. Gore flew on the designated Air Force One 747's. The crew was on President Clinton's last overseas mission to Ireland and the United Kingdom when the Supreme Court announced the ruling in Bush v Gore, finally bringing the Presidential Election of 2000 to an end. Vice President Gore won the national popular vote but lost the Electoral College vote.

My final campaign, the reelection campaign of George Bush was by far the most demanding. This was also the smallest winning margin for an incumbent President since Woodrow Wilson in the 1916 Presidential Election.

This was one of those campaigns that you kiss the wife and kids and say goodbye because we were going to be on the road for a while. This campaign is also where the President did a lot of

Airport Rallies. That is where we land, and everything goes silent. No power, no lights and no air conditioning while the President was speaking.

On Election Day of 2006, we started off in Waco Texas as the President voted in his hometown of Crawford, Texas. We then flew to an airport rally in Ohio and then on into Andrews, AFB in Maryland. When we landed at Andrews, the President and his daughters had a very tender moment in which they thought he was going to lose the election.

Later those tears of sorrow turned into cheers of celebration. Four more years.

Chewing the Rag with The President

President Clinton was on a nine-day trip to five different Cities in China. This was great for me because I got the opportunity to travel to several cities I had never been to before. One of those cities was Hong Kong. This was our final stop on this nine-day trip. Air Force One was the first international aircraft and first passengers to arrive at the airport, as it was only opened earlier in that day.

Although Hong Kong is known as the Pearl of the Orient, for me, the City was the New York City of the Far East. There was so much to do but so little time to do it. So, needless to say, by the time we got back to the aircraft, we were pretty tired. The worst part of that was we had an extremely long direct flight back to Andrews.

When we took off out of Hong Kong, we were scheduled for a 12-hour flight back. That meant that the flight attendants had an extremely long day ahead of us. Sometime during the flight when most of the passengers were asleep, President Clinton came back to the rear galley in a talkative mood. These were one and a million opportunities to get to sit and talk to the most powerful man in the world as if I was having a conversation with my friends.

It was extremely interesting giving the President a topic and just listening to him pontificate. Near the end of our chat session, I told the President that I too had political aspirations. President Clinton said, "Jeff, tell me about it."

So, I explained to President Clinton how Niagara Falls used to be the Honeymoon Capital of the World and how Bob Barker and the World used to come there for a few weeks for three years in a row to host the Miss USA pageant. I told him I wanted to go back to my hometown and become the Mayor. I said I wanted to use everything I had learned being around all these world leaders go back and help them get back to where they once were and make it a better place to live.

President Clinton said, "Jeff that is wonderful. I would love to help you with that."

I laughed, and said, "Mr. President, I am serious!"

President Clinton grabbed my hand looked me straight in the eyes and said, "Jeff, I am serious!"

I replied, "Thank you, Mr. President."

Prior to walking back up front, the President asked if I was bringing my family to the White House that evening to watch the 4th of July Fire Works from the White House Lawn. You see, the White House extends invitations to WH employees to view the fireworks from the South Lawn. They also provide drinks and ice cream. The AF-1 organization had been given tickets, however, they were given out while we were out on the road. I told the President that the tickets were already given out. President Clinton said, "You go up front and tell Lou that you and your family will be coming over tonight."

I said, "Yes Sir! And, thank you." My family and I had an outstanding time and a most wonderful view of the fireworks.

Putting My Faith to Work

As a young adult member of the Oxon Hill church of Christ, I had a lot of interaction with the youth of the congregation. Oxon Hill had one of the largest youth groups in the DC, MD VA area and they needed some young couples to interact with them. My wife and I along with another couple from Andrews AFB; Jim and Melissa Hengst volunteered.

As youth leaders we would entertain the youth at our residences for various get-togethers, serve as chaperones for events and mentor as needed. It seemed there were youth at my house more than I was there. But that was not a problem. We loved having them and they loved being there. Some of the many occasions I had the youth at my home for events like Movie Night, Birthdays and even Dress Up as Your Favorite Biblical Character Night. One of my favorite movies was the Western Film The Good, The Bad and The Ugly. We did this movie at least twice a year.

Youth Rallies were always wonderful events, and during the late 1980's they were very popular. The leadership at the Oxon Hill Church of Christ was aware of this and wanted to capitalize on it. They chartered a bus which filled up in no time at all, to go to the National Church of Christ Youth Rally at the Grand Ole Opry in Nashville, TN. I always participated in these trips, and we all had outstanding times, in spite of the 14 long hours on a bus, with 40-plus lively youth.

Once we arrived in Nashville, we were set up with accommodations on David Lipscomb University and witnessed several big stars that performed on stage at the Grand Ole Opry. We also had the opportunity to ride all day long at the theme park at Opryland. The congregation hosted this trip for three years in a row. I have some outstanding pictures of each of these trips, which I refer to as "adventures in youth."

In 1989, the congregation at Oxon Hill hosted a Youth Rally featuring Jeff Wallings who was an outstanding youth minister. There were youth from all over the East Coast coming. So many that the entire congregation had to open their homes to youth sleeping on floors and any extra beds. The auditorium was filled to capacity and Jeff Wallings did not let us down. He delivered some outstanding lessons and we were all truly edified.

The relationships we formed with the youth of the Oxon Hill Congregation still remain to this day. One of the youths, in particular, was having some troubles at home and consequently wanted to run away from home. We talked for a long time, and I gave him a quarter (as phone calls at that time were only 25 cents). I told him if he ever needed to talk, no matter what time it was, to give me a call. Gratefully, we have formed an outstanding big brother little brother relationship and he still has that quarter to this day.

JFK Career Days

Having such a great relationship with the youth of my church, it was an outstanding honor when I was first invited to the John F. Kennedy International Airport's Career Day by my good friend, Sonia. Sonia worked at one of the New York hotels that our AF1 crew often stayed at during President Clinton's travels. She was aware of my involvement with youth and suggested that they invite me to the Career Day.

AF1 Crew Giarrizzo, Elder, Powell and Joell

This annual event is put on by The Port Authority of New York and New Jersey, and held in a hangar on the massive JFK International Airport complex. Over 800 high school and junior high school inner city youth attend the event.,

With the approval of the AF-1 Commander, I loaded up with AF-1 picture packets and M&M's and proceeded to NYC. Another friend, Orlando, who worked for the Port Authority of NY, met me there. He was also a big part of the event. It was an amazing experience. I met some truly outstanding people, including members of the Tuskegee Airmen. That was a high point for me as I am a huge fan of their many accomplishments.

For me, there was always a sense of accomplishment, in doing what was needed to promote and perpetuate employment information about the industry I care about, to the youth of the

NYC region. The JFK International Airport's Career Days also allowed me to present myself as a positive African American role model. I kindly offer my gratitude to the organizers of this event for allowing me to participate on a yearly basis right up to my retirement from the United States Air Force.

RETIREMENT DINNER IN HONOR OF MSGT. JEFFREY ELDER
6 OCTOBER 2006

Part Seven

Closing Doors & Starting a New Chapter

Tuskegee Airmen

It was a special treat to be a part of the historic Tuskegee Airman's National Convention, held in Washington, DC in August 1998. I had long admired these brave men's courage and intellect, as the first black military aviators in the U.S. Army Air Corps (AAC), the precursor of the U.S. Air Force. The National Convention was August 4- 9, 1998. I had met some of the Airmen at New York Airport's Annual Aviation Career Day.

The convention events were coordinated by the Andrews AFB Protocol Team working in concert with the Tuskegee Airmen Inc. (TAI). Our goal was to ensure the success of the convention and enable the DV's to leave the Washington DC area with a very positive attitude about their host, TAI and the Air Force.

Jeff and J.C. Hayward

DC Airmen provided support as escorts, drivers, and information assistants. As a volunteer, I had no idea which assignment I would have, but was assigned as military escort for J. C. Hayward, D.C.'s WUSA Channel 9 news anchor who was Master of Ceremonies (MC) for the event.

This was not a hard assignment for me at all, for when I met Ms. Hayward, she made me feel as if I was the hero. It was an outstanding week and an honor to be a part of such a prestigious event.

Part Eight

Racquetball in my Veins

Racquetball

Racquetball has had a very special place in my heart for many years. When I first picked up a racquet at Sembach Air Base in Germany, I had no clue how deeply involved it would become in my life.

I played at Hancock Field, but it was actually at Homestead AFB in Florida in 1987, as I was playing racquetball with my good Friend, the Late Kenneth Green, Sr., that he encouraged me to enter my first tournament in the civilian community. It was at the Miami Lakes Club. That was it, I had the fever. Prior to that I was content with playing on Base and becoming the Base Champion.

When I transferred to Andrews AFB in Maryland, my racquetball career really took off. In 1988, Andrews had the best racquetball team in Command. At that time, the Base still had not only Air Force One but also what was known as Systems Command. Those two major Commands on one Base made the base huge when it came to personnel.

Prime Time on the racquetball court was from 11 a.m. – 1 p.m., lunch time. There were so many good players that we would race to get to the court and put our names on the challenge list. For winners, there was a two-game limit then you had to come off and put your name back on the list.

There were times when if you got beat and there were so many people on the list you just had to leave and go back to work. I had to compete with players like Bob Ryan, Pete Vaccaro, Rafael Ocasio and Mike Haywood just to name a few. Andrews was rich in talent.

The DC area is also where I started playing in state and national racquetball events. It was one thing to win on Base but when you competed off Base it was another level. We had a group of racquetball players from Bolling AFB which was known as the Dawg Pound.

The Dawg Pound had several men and women who were known throughout racquetball as some of the feistiest competitors around. When the Dawg Pound went to a tournament, many were destined to bring home some hardware.

Why the name Dawg Pound? Well, our greeting and salutations were a bark to each other. We all were also given Dawg Pound names. We had Atomic Dawg, Rasta Dawg and I was Snoop Dawg.

My mentor in racquetball was also a member of the Dawg Pound. Willie Sutton, also known as Papa Poon Dawg. We also called him Little Willie as we had two Willie Sutton's in our group. Papa Poon and a few others were at one time a part of the All Military Racquetball Team. Yes, there was an All Military Racquetball Team. Each service had its own team.

Military Racquetball

I had always wanted to be a part of this military gathering of racquetball players, but I couldn't get any recognition. That is, until I had a Sam Fox mission to the Air Force Academy. That is where I met the leading female racquetball player in the military and racquetball coach for the US Air Force Academy.

Captain Barbra Faulkenberry, (who later retired as a General), set up a time for us to play. When we finished, she asked why I had not been a part of the Air Force

racquetball team. I replied that nobody knows me. That was my last year not being known in not only Air Force racquetball but military racquetball. The very next year I received an invitation to compete at the All Air Force and All Military Racquetball

Championships hosted by Offutt, AFB near Omaha, Nebraska.

This championship is where I met, arguably, the best military racquetball player of all time Jimmy Lowe, and one of my best friends to this day Richard Eisemann, also known as Ice. Making it to the Show for the first time gave me the fever for military racquetball. As Ice put it, "I only had to win one more match and I would have made the Air Force Team." Had I won that match I would have gotten to stay for the next week to compete against the rest of the military in the Inter-service Racquetball Championships.

The following week, the All Military Team received an all-expense paid trip to the National Racquetball Championships in Houston Texas. That would have been three full weeks of racquetball, but I had to go back home for a week then use my own money to go to the Nationals only because I fell one match short. Never again!

In the following years, the All Military tournament was replaced by the Army Invitational Racquetball Championships hosted at the Fort Sam Houston Army Post in San Antonio, Texas. This was also known as the Military Nationals Racquetball Championships, sponsored by Wilson Sports. The Air Force would select players from their racquetball resumes and send them to these championships. We spent many extremely hot days competing at Fort Sam. That brings to mind the tournament in 1998.

The temperature was extremely hot early in the year and there were several forest fires burning out of control in Mexico. The extreme heat combined with the excessive amount of smoke coming up from the border created a health hazard. Many of the racquetball players were falling out due to exhaustion. Fortunately for me, I was in excellent physical condition that year and I was able to outlast many players that were better than I was. This was the only time that I beat Ice in competition. What a year!

The then Air Force Racquetball Team Coach/Captain, Joe Guyton was getting ready to retire. Joe asked me if I wanted to step in as the new Coach/Captain of the Air force Team. Of course, I said yes. That meant I would have to review all of the Air Force 303's (the Sports Resume Form) and recommend who would represent the Air Force at the All Army Invitational Tournament. Following this tournament, the military team would take a convoy from San Antonio to Houston to compete in the Nationals. Now only two full weeks of racquetball.

In 2001, one of the Air Force racquetball players from Europe, Will Smith; not to be confused with the actor, came to Fort Sam and was talking about a tournament in Ireland that he had just competed in, the Irish Open in Arklow, Ireland. Smitty, as we called him, kept going on about the hospitality and how well this tournament was run. I finally said, "Next year I am going to this Irish Open." That is exactly what I did. After all, being the Air Force Coach/Captain, this would give me a chance to view some of the Air Force players that live in Europe that had hopes of coming to Fort Sam for the All Army Invitational.

I didn't do so great in the tournament, but I did have an outstanding time. All of the Irish people rolled out the red carpet for the Foreigners who took time to come to their Country. We were so well received that I attended the Irish Open for the next ten years. It was like I became a celebrity in Arklow. The Arklow Mayor would start the tournament each year and would call out, "Where is Jeffrey?" I still have many friends from those tournaments to this day.

I had been sponsored by the racquet company E-Force for a little while, which was great as with my last name Elder, I used to call it Elder Force. Then the person who sponsored me, Ron Halloran, developed his own racquet company and named it Gemini. Ron would have me stress test all his new equipment before it was ready for sale and given to other sponsored players. Ron worked very closely with Jon Perry who was an outstanding racquet stringer and fellow Air Force member. Jon is the reason I even got sponsored by Ron.

The company Gemini had some successes for a few years but in the racquet industry it's very hard to do well enough to survive for a prolonged period of time. As the end of Gemini was near, Ron told me to look for another sponsor.

Wilson Sports Kris and Terri

After Gemini sponsored me, Wilson Racquets Sports had their eyes on me. The two people running the racquetball program was Chris Evon and Terri Graham. When Chris and Terri approached me regarding a sponsorship, they asked what I wanted. My response was a full sponsorship for not only myself but also one for my co-harts in crime, the Iceman, who already had a partial paid sponsorship with Wilson. They agreed and thus started a relationship that I can't even put into words. These two women became like family to not only me and Ice but when my daughters started playing, they looked at them as their family also.

We always looked forward to the National events where we knew we would all get to hang out. Wilson was a major sponsor to the sport of racquetball and took great interest in the military and National Juniors' Programs.

Chris and Terri are now extremely instrumental in National Pickle Ball becoming just as popular, as they host the Minto, US OPEN National Pickleball Championships. On behalf of all the Sponsored Wilson racquetball players and now pickleball players; thank you Chris and Terri for everything and for just being you.

Willie D.

I would often play racquetball on the Fort Myer Army Post to meet different players and keep my game toned. One of the players at Ft. Myer was none other than the late Willie Davenport. Willie Davenport, a Colonel in the Army National Guard won an Olympic Gold Medal in the 110-meter high hurdles at the 1968 Summer Olympics in Mexico City, Mexico. He also won a Bronze Medal in the same event eight years later in Montreal, Canada. Willie, as he liked to be called, wasn't the greatest racquetball player but he was an outstanding athlete and a politician of sorts.

One year, the All Army Invitational had been set and orders had been sent out. Then, due to funding the Army cancelled the tournament and rescinded the orders. Willie as always, brought to the courts some influential people. This time he had with him the Sergeant Major of the Army who liked to dabble in racquetball. When Willie introduced him to me, I told the Sergeant Major that we had met a few weeks earlier when he was among the President's guests aboard Air Force One.

The Sergeant Major thanked me for the wonderful hospitality afforded to him on his flight. We somehow got on the subject of the All Army Invitational racquetball tournament that had just been cancelled. When the Sergeant Major heard that the Army rescinded the orders, he was not pleased. "This issue is dealing with the moral and welfare of my troops," he said.

He asked that we provide him with the particulars and that he would check into it. As it turned out, the Sergeant Major of the Army has some clout. The next week the tournament had been turned back on and orders were reissued. I gathered an Air Force team in a very short time, and we all participated in and thoroughly enjoyed what was to be the last All Military Racquetball Championship. Thank you, Sergeant Major of the

Army Jack L. Tilley, and rest in peace Willie D. Davenport.

USA Racquetball Board of Directors

One of our military players Frank Taddonio, Colonel, United States Army, who also assisted in providing information to the Sergeant Major of the Army, was on the USA Racquetball's Board of Directors as the Military Representative. USA Racquetball (USAR) is the National Governing Body for the sport of racquetball, recognized by the U.S. Olympic Committee and is committed to excellence and service to its members. The Colonel was getting ready to deploy downrange and needed someone to replace him as the military representative on the BOD. He asked me if I would be interested in the position and I gladly accepted.

Being on the USA Board of Directors was a very demanding, time consuming thing. With the conference calls, in-face meetings and, depending on which committee you were on, free time was something that I didn't have much of. But it was so worth it. Racquetball is my love and being right in the middle of everything was great.

As the Military Representative on the BOD, I represented the entire military. This also allowed us to have military presence at all major racquetball events. The National Championships each year was usually our biggest event, and we would have all military players come out on stage in their service dress uniform and receive a tribute. This became a highlight for many, both military and civilian racquetball players.

USA Racquetball's Headquarters is in Colorado Springs, Colorado. That is also where the U.S. Olympic Training Center is located. Because USAR falls under the U. S. Olympic Committee, the board members and professional athletes are allowed to utilize the facilities at the Olympic Training Center. On occasion, Olympic athletes would be brought in during special meetings and we were able to mingle with them.

On one such occasion, several times Olympic Gold Medalist, Michael Johnson was brought in. When he found out that I was a crew member on Air Force One he was extremely interested and wanted to hear about what it was like flying around the world with the most powerful person in the world. He was a big President Clinton fan. On the other hand, I was inquiring about those Gold Shoes. We had some good laughs together talking about our experiences.

Racquetball Tours

I wasn't the greatest racquetball player by no means; but I knew all of the top players in the World. Being a member of the President's crew on AF-1 had many privileges. One of those privileges was that we could provide friends and family members tours of the plane when we were either at Andrews or on the road. I was the connection for the racquetball community to this privilege. I didn't want to abuse this privilege, but I did use it a lot as I had friends and family all over the world.

Some of my best tours of AF-1 for the racquetball community were of course The Iceman and his family, Chris and Terri from Wilson Sports and their families, Derek "Big D." Robinson and his family, Cliff Swain and Rocky Carson and his family.

Rocky Carson has been one of my favorite racquet ballers. He is one of the greatest racquetball players in the world; being a five-time Men's Singles World Champion. This is still an International Racquetball Federation career record, and at the time he was the current Pan Am Games Champion in Men's Singles.

I will always remember the day that I gave Rocky and his family the tour. That is because it is also the same day of The Northeast blackout of 2003. The date was August 14, 2003, and AF-1 was on a West Coast swing with President Bush.

Rocky and his family came out and we were enjoying a wonderful tour of the plane when the word went out that something was going on back on the East Coast. Not knowing if there was a terrorist nexus, we had to stop the tour and were put on alert. Thank goodness, we were just about finished with the tour and were just hanging out. I got to spend some great time with them. Experiences like this one are among the ones that I enjoyed most during my career on AF-1.

Some of the things that I really enjoyed about Rocky were, the first thing he always does after a competition is to give thanks to God for allowing him to be able to compete. Also, Rocky never let his fame go to his head. I have always talked about writing a book about my AF-1 adventures and Rocky has expressed interest in writing a book about his career. Rocky, I implore you to put your story in print. I will be in line for the first copy. Thanks to you and your family for such great friendship, and continued success both on and off the court.

Family Racquetball

I recall playing in my first Maryland State Racquetball Championships in 1991. I made it to the finals of the Men's 25+ B. My opponent was none other than Frank Finich, a guy originally from Buffalo, NY. This was the first time Frank and I had come across each other although we knew of each other. All of my Dawg Poundsters were also in attendance to root me on and as many of them were also there to play in their finals.

I came out on top of the first game and Frank came up with the second. That meant that we had to go to a tiebreaker.

To get to the finals we both had to play several long matches and we both were feeling as if we had been in a marathon.

At the beginning of the tiebreaker, I started cramping up. The cramps looked like grapefruits in each leg. Cramping is usually a sign of poor conditioning. However, that was not the case for me. I was in great condition, unfortunately I just had to play so many matches because I was playing in two divisions.

I only had two 30 second time outs which I took. I think I milked them both just a little. Laura Patterson, a member of our Dawg Pound put some Therapeutic Mineral Ice on my affected areas and massaged it in. I was able to continue.

Not long after that Frank started cramping. I knew exactly what he was going through having just been there; so, Laura gave him the same treatment and he was able to continue. The score went back and forth and we both wound up at 10 to 10 in a first to 11 game. We both were just looking for anything that would get us over the hump. There was a huge crowd around watching as all of the Dawg Poundsters and us players were making a lot of noise.

Dianna was there, as always, cheering me on. She said, "Come on Jeff, let's go."

Then, out of nowhere my baby Brianna said, "Daddy," clapping her hands. I went to the service box and served an ace to end the match. The entire crowd erupted with applause. Frank and I embraced for a long time. He then told me and the crowd that I need to bottle that moment that my daughter inspired me to take it out.

That was my very first Maryland State Championship win. Frank and I have battled many times since then going back and forth.

The friendship that we share is a wonderful thing and we both look back on that as a wonderful moment.

We know how passionate I am about racquetball, but it was a special treat when my daughters started playing. It all started at the Dawg Pound. I would take my daughter Brianna or Munch, with me every day as her mother was working and there is no way that I was going to pay for a babysitter. After all, Munch was my shadow. Every time I made a move to go somewhere, she thought she was supposed to go, and most of the time she did. At the Dawg Pound it was like everybody was family so anytime one of us brought our children around, all pitched in looking out for them.

Like Father, Like Daughter

One day when entering the Dawg Pound, I did my traditional greeting and salutations bark, and Munch close behind me gave a little bark. The whole Dawg Pound erupted with laughter. They said, "She is a true Dawg Poundster, now."

Not long after that one day, Munch accompanied me to the court as usual. And just as I was walking onto the court, she asked, "Daddy, can I play?"

I said, "WHAT? Of course, you can."

There was an empty court and I was thinking that it would tire her out before we got home. I gave her a set of goggles, a racquet and a sporty head band. She was set for action.

I went on the court and hit the ball with her for a little while then told her to practice what I taught her. After some time, Munch came out and said, "Whew Daddy, that was fun!" I then thought to myself, *I got her*! Family racquetball had begun. From then on, every day that I went to play, I had to ensure that there was a court on which Munch could play.

I put her in her first tournament when she was six years old. For that age they played multi-bounce, meaning that the ball could bounce two times before you had to hit it. I quickly found out that the apple doesn't fall far from the tree. Munch had that same competitive nature that I have. From that point on, when I signed up for a tournament and they had a junior's event; I signed Munch up also.

I took Munch to her first Jr. National Championships in June of 2001, held at the Lakewood Athletic Club in Denver, Colorado. I remember those dates very well because National Geographic had just completed a documentary on Air Force One and it was going to premier in Downtown Washington, DC, during the same time.

I had a decision to make, do I go to the National Geographic Premier or take my baby to her first Junior National Racquetball Championships. This was not a tough decision, I was taking my baby to the Nationals. I wanted her to experience what it's like at a competition at the top level in the Country for youth.

This was our very first outing together for family racquetball. We both had an outstanding time although I think I had even more fun than Munch. You see, I was newly elected to the USA Racquetball Board of Directors as the Military Representative and the Juniors' Program was one of the committees I was assigned to.

The level of play was much better than Munch, but she hung in there like a trooper. I also have to thank Danielle Keys who was assigned as Munch's double partner. Danielle was a more advanced player, but she helped Munch navigate through the matches with patience and dignity. Both of the Keys girls, Danielle and her older sister Michele, could play some mean racquetball. This family outing gave me and Munch a great opportunity to bond around a sport that I truly loved and was hoping that she loved also.

Of course, Danielle, or "Snookums", wanted to play after she saw Munch play racquetball with me all the time. One day she asked, "Daddy, when can I start playing?" What could I say? I gave her some equipment and showed her the ropes. Like her big sister, she greatly enjoyed playing and was anxious to play in tournaments. I told Snook that when she turns six I would put her in her first tournament just as I did with Munch.

Snook's first tournament was the Regional Championships in March of 2002, at the Severna Park Racquetball and Fitness Club located in Severna Park, Maryland State. This was a great place to start because they offered events for all ages. This is also the first time we all competed in a tournament together. Now, my girls had the fever just as I did.

The next event was the Junior Nationals in Nashua, New Hampshire. Both girls came home with medals. Because I was on the USA Racquetball's Board of Directors and a part of the juniors committee, I had to be at the tournaments anyway, so, it was just gravy that I had my girls there also playing. Wilson Sports sponsored me, so I dressed my girls in the Wilson brand also. Chris and Terri from Wilson treated my girls the same way they treated me, outstanding. Next up was the Junior Worlds Championships.

Junior Worlds

In December of 2003, the United States of America hosted the Junior Worlds Racquetball Championships in Orlando Florida. This was an opportunity for my girls to play racquetball on the International stage. I would incorporate my vacations into the times when my girls had tournaments. Yes, I had official duties while at Junior Worlds as a Board of Directors member, but ensuring my babies had an outstanding time and got to meet some new friends was my top priority.

Both of my girls came home with medals and the best part was that they met some new friends from all over the world. Just watching them interact in the International arena warmed my heart.

Following the Jr. Worlds, me and both of my girls found our names in the age group National Rankings in Racquetball Magazine. We were all in the top ten in the country at the same time. Brianna, #10, Danielle #2 and I was # 1 in our skilled age division.

Shnurman Family

Snook had made some new friends because they had a very little puppy in a bag. I went over to meet them and felt an instant connection. It was Harry Shnurman and his family, and the little puppy was called "Heavy Duty." The Shnurman family was from Prole, Iowa and they had driven their motor home down to Orlando for the junior world racquetball championships.

Harry and I instantly formed a friendship and during the tournament week his family and mine hung out a lot. The cool part was we both took great pride in teaching our children the finer aspects of life to include racquetball.

Harry and I would team up in the mornings and play other

parents before the International competition would start. I

have to say that Harry was a very good player. At the end of the tournament Harry asked me if my family would be attending the Junior Nationals the next year which were to take place in Eau Claire, Wisconsin. I said yes and he then invited me and my family to come to his family farm in Iowa after the tournament. I gave him a conditional answer of yes.

The following year at the Junior Nationals in Eau Claire, Wisconsin; Harry and I picked up right where we left off. We would team up and take on all parent challengers early in the mornings. We were a force to be reckoned with. It was a lot of fun for us, but the tournaments were all about our children and we ensured that they had outstanding times while playing the game that we all truly loved.

At the end of Junior Nationals, we packed up our vehicles and followed Harry and his family back to Iowa. Along the ride there we had an interesting thing happen. We were driving through all these little towns and then we found ourselves in the middle of a parade. Harry and I have no idea how it happened but all of a sudden, we were waving at people and they were expecting us to throw them candy. We stopped at a gas station nearby and just talked about what just happened. This was hilarious.

When we arrived at Harry's home and farm in Prole, IA; my family's vacation continued. But for Harry's family, it was time to get back to work. All of his family members had specific duties and living on a farm is no joke. I had no idea how much stuff has to be done on a daily basis. Harry and Charlotte were dedicated to creating a self-sustaining, independent, and carefree life for their family. Nearly everything they ate came from their farm.

This was very exciting for my girls as they grew up in the city and had never experienced farm life. We even helped out with all of the chores. Well, nearly all of the chores. One day Harry said, "Tomorrow we will be prepping the chickens." I knew what that meant and when I told my daughters they insisted on sleeping in that morning, and they did.

Now just because I knew what they were going to do doesn't mean that I had done it before. They all were very patient showing me the ropes. This turned out to be a great experience and an outstanding vacation.

All of the Shnurman family members had extremely long hair. All of my family had long hair except me. So, Harry gave me a hat to wear that had a long blonde ponytail attached, to make sure I didn't feel out of place. Harry and his family were excellent hosts. Thank you to the Shnurman family for making this a memorial time for my family.

About a year after our vacation, we had an AF-1 mission to Des Moines, IA. I contacted Harry and the family and invited them to come out for a tour of AF-1. It was great to see them and enjoy just a little time together. As it turned out, that would be the last time I ever saw Harry. In January of 2007, Harry died of a heart attack on his farm. This was devastating news. Most regrettable was that I could not attend his funeral. Harry and I were two totally different people. We looked nothing alike but the two things we had very much in common was the Love for our families and the sport of racquetball. We had a friendship that I wish lasted much longer. Rest in peace my friend.

Oh, the People You Meet

I can take little credit for my good luck in meeting some of the most sought-after celebrities in the world. It was all about the company I kept. The same way I was in awe at some of the big names, the stars and celebrities always seemed to be in awe of the Presidents and First Ladies that we served. The fact that we had the opportunity to rub shoulders with the beautiful stars was simply a perk for working for the most powerful leaders in the world.

I must say that I was always surprised that the men and women who most of us view as isolated from everyday people, were surprisingly down to earth and approachable. They were often as interested in our lives as we were in theirs. Those that lived up to the expectations of being out of reach… their loss, not ours.

Traveling around the world on Presidential missions, we were bound to meet a lot of world leaders but also many celebrities. More than any other President, President Clinton seemed to attract the most celebrities inside and outside the country. There was something star-like about him that drew people in.

The following are a few of my personal experiences during my service to our country.

James Brown

I was on an out and back to Groton, CT First Lady Mission on the C-9 aircraft. Vance and Dean were the AF-1 flight attendants, and Jackie Brown and I were from the 99th.

While on our ground stop, I saw a stretch Limousine pull up next to our aircraft. As everybody started speculating as to who it was for, I said, "I'll go out and find out."

I approached the limo and asked the driver who he was waiting for. He replied, "The God Father of Soul, Mr. James Brown." So, I went back to our aircraft and told them who was going to be landing next to us.

Many of the crew from the C-9 wanted to meet him and I was elected the Ambassador to see if he was interested in touring the First Lady's aircraft. When I went out and talked to the driver again who had communication with Mr. Brown's aircraft, he told me that, yes, Mr. Brown would like to stop by. When I went back and told the crew that Mr.

Brown would be stopping by after he lands, some of the crew was doubtful he really would.

But true to form, when Mr. Brown's aircraft landed, the limo driver picked him up and drove him around to the First Lady's C-9. The entire C-9 crew was elated. Mr. Brown got out of the limo in a bright green body suit and the first thing that he said was, "Oh, I feel good!"

Of course, I greeted him and thanked him for giving us some of his time. Mr. Brown got a brief tour of the C-9 and took pictures with the crew members. Right before he left, Mr. Brown gave me a CD called *The Greatest Hits of the Fourth Decade*. To this day I have not opened that CD, but I have listened to all of the songs on it.

Tiger Woods

In 1996, President Clinton was on a trip through the Pacific to attend the APEC Summit Meeting in Manila, Philippines. However, our first stop was in Australia. This was my first time visiting this Country and I was very excited to be there.

As we always do, the crew had dinner together at a fine restaurant. After my meal I went to the rest room and as I was going past the entrance, I noticed a young man that resembled Tiger Woods. After I came out of the rest room my curiosity was still getting the best of me, so I went to the doorman and asked if that was indeed Tiger.

The doorman said, "Yes, that was Tiger."

I immediately ran out the door just in time to see Tiger and two other gentlemen going into the club next door. This club had a healthy entry fee that I was not interested in paying, but I went to the doorman anyway and asked if Tiger had just entered.

The doorman replied, "Yes, are you a friend of Tiger?" Before I had a chance to answer, he said, "Go ahead in Mate."

I replied, "Just a minute, I have some more friends next door that would like to come also."

The doorman replied, "Okay, go and get them."

When I got back to the restaurant, I told the guys, "Hey, we are in next doors. Come on."

When we all arrived back at the club we were greeted by the doorman and he kindly let us in. Once in, we were not thinking about Tiger. We all just started having a great time like we just took over the place. Tiger noticed us from across the floor and I motioned him over. He asked, "What are all you Americans doing here?"

I explained that we were part of the Presidential crew on AF-1 for President Clinton. He thought that was great. Tiger told us that he was there to golf against Greg Norman. He then asked what we were drinking, and we thought he was about to order a round of drinks. But he followed that up with a question. "What do you think I should drink?" One of our guys said, "You might want a rum and coke." So that is what he had.

We all had an outstanding time that night that lasted well into the morning. In fact, the sun was out when we went back to our hotel. As for Tiger, He did give out one autograph that evening, and it was to me. However, his golfing with Mr. Norman didn't go so well.

King Hussein

In March of 1996, President Clinton invited King Hussein of Jordan to fly on AF-1 with him to Egypt for the Summit of the Peacemakers March. Of course, the King had a very nice airplane of his own, but it gave him and President Clinton some good time together.

King Hussein was an extremely pleasant man as he came through the aircraft and greeted some of the crew members. We had the opportunity to chat for a little while and I told him that I had previously been to Amman Jordan and he asked, "How was your experience?"

I told him that I had a wonderful time there and that I looked forward to visiting his country again. The King was very pleased. To my knowledge, he and his security team were the only ones to smoke on the 747, AF-1.

Henry Winkler

On one of our first trips to California with President Clinton, Henry Winkler came out for a meet and greet with the President. Afterwards he stayed around for a tour of AF-1.

Mr. Winkler had a great time getting to know the crew. We all wanted to take photos with him but that wasn't the normal protocol. Mr. Winkler, sensing that was the case, said, "Hey, why don't we take photos, two people at a time?" We all agreed, and had a wonderful time snapping the photos with the Fonz.

At the end of his tour, Mr. Winkler called every crew member that he met by our first and last name. I thought that was incredible. Not only did we get the pictures of us with him two at a time, but Mr. Winkler also sent us autographed studio photos of him and autographed Fonzie photos signed to each individual. I think he had as good a time with us as we did with him.

Arsenio Hall and Edward James Olmos

Arsenio Hall and Edward James Olmos accompanied President Clinton on a trip to Los Angeles. The Arsenio Hall Show had been extremely popular from 1989 until 1994 and the crew enjoyed having some laughs onboard with him.

I had been a huge fan of Mr. Olmos ever since his Miami Vice days as Lt. Martin Castillo. You see at the time when Miami Vice first premiered, I was stationed at Homestead AFB in Florida and this show was the talk of the town. In fact, it was reported that crime in the city of Miami was at record lows during the premieres.

Miami Vice also had everybody sporting the latest styles of sport coats and t shirts. So, it was a pleasure to get to talk to him and relate my Miami Vice experiences. At the end of the flight Mr. Olmos gave me an autographed note on Aboard Air Force One paper saying, "Jeff, Great food, Great flight. Edward James Olmos, 7-10-99."

Cuba Gooding Jr.

On a West Coast trip with President Clinton, me and a couple other flight attendants went to lunch at of all places, Hooters. Well, I am from Niagara Falls, right next to Buffalo where chicken wings were first served. As we were sitting there, I looked around and said to Rob, one of my coworkers, "I think that is Cuba Gooding, Jr."

I said, "I'm going over to see if it is him." As I got closer, I noticed that it was indeed Mr. Gooding. As we struck up a conversation, I told him that I had met his father, Cuba Gooding Sr. about a month prior. Cuba Gooding Sr. was the lead singer of the soul group, "The Main Ingredient." He and his band brought the house down at the La Louisanne Restaurant and Night Club in Los Angeles.

Cuba Gooding and I chatted for a while then I asked if he would take a photo with me. He agreed but insisted that nothing be in the background saying Hooters. I totally agreed.

Senator John Glenn

On October 29, 1998, the AF-1 crew received a treat of lifetime proportion. Not long after landing at the Cape Canaveral Air Station skid strip with President Clinton, we got to view the launch of Senator John Glenn's return to space after 50 years onboard the Space Shuttle Discovery.

Not long prior to this mission, President Clinton had John Glenn as a guest onboard AF-1. The Senator met the entire AF-1 crew and gave us Limited edition Challenge Coins commemorating mission Mercury-Atlas VI, being the first American to orbit the earth and mission STS-95, on the Space Shuttle Discovery, his return to space at the age of 77 years old. This was truly an honor.

Chris Tucker

During the 1990's Chris Tucker was an extremely popular entertainer. Known for his standup comedy routines and several breakout movies; so, it was great to find out that he would be greeting President Clinton as AF-1 arrived in Los Angeles on a trip.

The crew was told that Mr. Tucker would hang around the aircraft for a while after the President departed for a tour and to mingle with crew members. And that is what he did. Mr. Tucker had fun messing with everybody. He had a camera crew with him as he was making a movie of him being the President.

Mr. Tucker even tried to mess with the Secret Service as he walked toward the President's limo waving as if he was the President. But one look from the Secret Service Agent at the limo let him know that he was not going to get any closer.

So much for his camera crew filming that scene.

Mr. Tucker came up behind one of the flight crew chiefs and he was wiping down the stairs and said to him, "Yo man. Is this what you do when everybody is gone?" The crew chief looked up at him, and Mr. Tucker said, "I'm just playing, man!" We all laughed, and he proceeded on to the next victim.

Before Mr. Tucker departed the aircraft, he ensured that he took pictures with everybody that wanted to. The photo that I took with Mr. Tucker in front of AF-1 turned out to be more important than I could have ever imagined. My niece, Latoya, who has Lupus, became gravely ill and was hospitalized for an extended time. I knew she was a huge Chris Tucker fan, and I was also one of her favorite people, so I put the picture of Chris Tucker and me up over her bed as we were watching over her.

Jeff keeps promise to Latoya for WH Tour

Prior to her having a breathing tube placed in, I asked her, "If you get up out of this bed and recover what would you want me to do?" Latoya replied that she would like to be taken to the White House. My reply was, "'Nough Said!"

Remarkably, and after much prayer, Latoya made a full recovery. And one of the best things is that she doesn't even remember having that breathing tube in her, which caused her so much discomfort.

True to form, I scheduled a time for Latoya to come to Maryland and visit my family. I also reached out to Glenn Powell who is an outstanding friend and worked at the White House Transportation Agency (WHTA). Glenn was in charge of ensuring that all passengers on AF-1 had their bags when they arrived at their hotels. Glenn was very good at what he did. He was so good that he wrote a book about it.

When I reached out to him and told him how my niece wanted to go to the White House, Glenn set everything up. My family and Glenn's family toured the White house together. Oh, we got the fifty cents tour. My girls and niece even got to play with the Clinton's cat, Socks. My niece was extremely pleased. Mission accomplished.

Rocky Carrol

Most everyone knows what POTUS means—President of the United States of America. Well, Rocky Carroll was known as BOTUS, Bootmaker of the United States of America. He received that unofficial distinction because he has made custom boots for the past seven Presidents.

Mr. Carroll flew on AF-1 on occasion and when we met, he told me that he would one day make a pair of boots for me. He took the measurements of my feet and that was it. I had forgotten about it but sometime later I received a package from Mr. Carroll with my custom-made boots that had the Presidential Seal and even had my monogramed initials on them. The boots fit like a glove. I almost didn't want to wear them for fear of messing them up. But when I did wear them, I wore them with pride. After all, not everyone can say that they were wearing custom boots made by the bootmaker to the Presidents.

Kenny G

President Clinton would often go to the Caribbean during the Christmas Holidays, and to bring in the New Year. The backup aircraft would leave on New Year's Day and go to Puerto Rico for almost a week. I preferred this trip as it allowed me to be home with my family on Christmas Day and to celebrate New Year's Eve. What could be better?

Leaving Washington, DC in January to spend nearly a week in Puerto Rico and having no official duties other than rest and relaxation. Um, sign me up!

The crew stayed at a very nice hotel. One of my first nights there I ventured to the Grand Hotel next door to where we were staying. They had a casino and I always liked to watch people gamble their money away. As I was watching, this one guy's lights started going off and bells started ringing. I was curious to find out what he had won. Well after the bells and lights going off for several minutes and nobody coming, I went to find a casino worker to assist.

Upon my return with a casino worker, the man at the slot machine thanked me for helping as he introduced himself. He then asked me if I liked the musician Kenny G. I replied, "Of course! He's great."

Mr. Littleton then asked if I would be interested in attending the Kenny G concert at the Roberto Clemente Coliseum the next day. As it turned out, Mr. Littleton was the Production Manager of Kenny G. I said yes, and he told me that two tickets would be at Will Call with my name on them.

When I returned to our hotel, I saw Steve who was running our Backup mission. I told him of my experience, and he said that he would like to attend the concert with me. So, the next day Steve and I made our way to the Roberto Clemente Coliseum Box Office. There I was handed an envelope which had two VIP tickets with backstage access.

Steve and I looked at each other and said we are in the house as we preceded backstage. There we were met by Mr. Littleton. We got to meet the band members and other VIP ticket holders. This was my first backstage experience. Mr. Littleton told us we would also be able to come backstage after the concert and at that time we will get to meet Kenny G. Then, we were escorted to our front row seats.

The lights went down and as he often does, Kenny G started off his concert holding a note somewhere in the audience.

Then the spotlight appeared on him as he made his way to he stage still holding that note. You see, Kenny G was in the Guinness Book of World Records for holding the longest note on a wind instrument using the technique called circular breathing.

Once Kenny G got to the stage, he continued the song that he started to a standing ovation. He had the Coliseum rocking. At the end of the concert, Steve and I made our way backstage and were introduced to Kenny G. We told him that we were part of the Presidential Crew on AF-1 and he told us that he was a huge fan of President Clinton. We then took pictures and ate some food with other band members. Kenny G signed some of his CDs and also gave us one for President Clinton.

Dale Earnhardt Jr.

Just looking at me, most people would never guess I am your average NASCAR fan. But quite the contrary. I love NASCAR racing. My daughter would sit in amazement that I could watch a full race and be fascinated straight through to the finish. My favorite driver was Dale Earnhardt Sr., also known as *The Intimidator*. His car was the black #3 Mr. Goodwrench Chevrolet. I also liked his son Dale Earnhardt, Jr., as he was a chip off the old block. I had an opportunity to see Dale, Jr. race; but unfortunately, I never saw Dale Sr. race in person.

I will never forget watching the Daytona 500 in February of 2001. I was in Waco, Texas watching the race in my hotel room. My best friend Ice and I were competitors as he was rooting for Dale Jarrett and I was rooting for Dale Earnhardt Sr.

Nearing the end of the race, things appeared all in my favor as number 1 was Michael Waltrip, 2 was Dale Earnhardt Jr. and 3 was Dale Sr. They were all on the same team. I was sitting on the edge of my bed with anticipation for the big win. Then in the final turn out of nowhere, a serious accident occurred. Dale Sr. was into the wall and hard.

I was on the phone with Ice when the accident occurred and we both didn't think that it was too bad. It was a very good and exciting race, and I was happy with the outcome of Michael Waltrip winning and Dale Jr. coming in second. Ice and I hung up and I headed out to get a bite to eat with other crew members.

It was a few hours later, that Ice called me to see how I was doing. As we talked about the race, he realized that I was not aware of the condition of Dale Sr. Ice said, "Jeff, he died!"

Hearing that, I felt as if I had lost a very close friend. This was a man that I had never met but the news of his death really hit me hard. At that time, Ice and I had extremely tight relationship. He totally understood how I felt and as we talked, I felt a little better.

President Bush, who was also a NASCAR fan, and considered Earnhardt and his wife Teresa to be friends, reached out to the Earnhardt family to express his condolences. A short while later a Presidential trip was scheduled to Charlotte, NC. President Bush invited the Earnhardt family out for a meet and greet. The Earnhardt family members were wife Teresa, sons Dale Jr. and Kerry, plus daughter Kelley.

Following the meet and greet, I was allowed to give the Earnhardt family a tour of Air Force One. Of course, this was a special treat for me as I was a huge fan of Dale Sr. and now Dale Jr. At the end of the tour, we took some pictures and Dale Jr. signed some autographs. This was an outstanding moment for me.

Carrol Shelby

In 2002, President Bush traveled to Texas often and the crew would stay in Waco for a few weeks at a time. On this particular visit, Ice invited me to attend the Samsung/RadioShack 500 NASCAR race at the Texas Motor Speedway in Fort Worth. Ice worked for Dr. Pepper at the time and their company had a racecar in the Sprint Race.

Dr. Pepper had a group of seats for its employees. As we were there enjoying ourselves, I went to the rest room. As I exited the restroom, I came in contact with a gentleman who noticed the shirt that I was wearing that said Presidential Crew, Air Force One. He asked me if my shirt was real and I said, "Yes, I am a member of the crew."

We talked for a few minutes and then he invited me up to their suite and wanted to introduce me to someone. After arriving to the suite, he introduced me to the one and only Carroll Shelby. Yes, the same Carroll Shelby, American automotive designer, racing driver and entrepreneur.

I was elated, for I am the owner of a classic 1966 Mustang Convertible. No, not a Shelby Mustang but still this was an honor. We got to chat for a while and before I left, Mr. Shelby gave me a 50th edition Mustang cap. He said, "Here is one for you and one for President Bush." I think everybody in Texas loved the Bush family, and they always extended a hearty welcome to his AF-1 crew.

Jeff and Brian Williams

There have been several news personnel that I had delightful times with on AF-1. Such as Peter Jennings and Brian Williams who would always come to the rear galley and take pictures with us. But I would also truly enjoy Ann Compton. Anytime Ms. Compton would see me no matter where we were, she would always make a point to come over and say hi and talk.

The AF-1 crew was invited to the State House in Little Rock when President Clinton was re-elected, and Ms. Compton saw us there and went out of her way to come over and converse

Jeff and Peter Jennings

with us. By the way, Ann Compton was also on AF-1 with us the whole day on September 11, 2001 and did an outstanding job of getting the story out.

Daddy's Almost Home

I was just about to leave the house, heading to the Air Force One Hangar to travel to Europe for a weeklong trip, and Dianna handed me a card. As I opened the card it had a little baby bootie in it. I looked at her and she said, "Are you ready to be a Daddy again?" I was floored!

Needless to say, I was late getting to the plane after that. When I arrived, my Chief came to me and said, "Jeff, what is going on? You know we can't be late." I then told him that Dianna told me that she was having a baby just before I left the house. He immediately asked, "Are you okay? Take as much time as you need." It's not that I didn't want another baby, it was just a big surprise.

A few days into the trip, I received a call from home stating that Dianna was having complications with the pregnancy and by all accounts, she was losing the baby. Being all the way over in Europe, I couldn't help her much. However, things settled down and our baby kept growing.

My nephew who lived in Niagara Falls came down to visit for the summer and help out while I was traveling. This was in 1996 and the Olympics were due to open in Atlanta.

President Clinton was to fly down for the day and be a part of the Opening Ceremonies. Dianna's due date was over a week away, so I thought I definitely wanted to be on this trip. After all, it was just for the day.

When we arrived in Atlanta, the crew was provided with hotel rooms for the day. That allowed us to change out of our suits and get out and enjoy some of the Olympic festivities. Around 11 a.m., I received a message on my beeper from the White House Communications Agency (WHCA) stating that my wife's water broke while at Walmart and that she was in transit to the hospital at Andrews AFB. I was thinking to myself: What are the chances of this happening?

Well, WHCA continued to provide me with updates throughout the day. The time came for our original departure to return to Andrews, the President was nowhere to be found. Yes, we were going to be late coming back. Just my luck. When the President did return, First Lady Hillary and Chelsea came on the plane. I was working in the forward galley and the First Lady saw me and said, "I hear somebody's in labor." I wasn't even aware that they knew what was going on.

I said, "Yes." And then the First Lady reflected on when Chelsea was born. When the President came aboard the aircraft, he said to Colonel Barr, "Let's get this plane back to Andrews so Jeff can be there for the birth of his child." The President then joined his wife and daughter in reflecting on when Chelsea was born.

Usually, the flight from Atlanta to Andrews takes about an hour and a half. This night Colonel Barr made it in an hour and five minutes. Not that I was counting or anything. When we landed, it was raining cats and dogs outside. The President was in the Conference Room upon landing and was walking back up to his cabin when he saw me.

President Clinton said, "Jeff, what are you still doing here?"

I said, "Mr. President, proper protocol. You leave, then we leave."

He said, "Get going."

I looked up the stairs at Colonel Barr, and he said, "You heard the man." I ran down the stairs of the aircraft and they had an aircrew vehicle waiting for me. They whisked me over to the hospital on base.

When I arrived, I was running through the hospital in my suit like OJ Simpson used to run through the airports in the old rental car commercials. When I got to the room, I opened the door and the first thing that I saw was this look that I will never forget. Dianna gave me one of those up, over and around looks. I then heard my baby cry. I immediately asked, "What do we have?"

Dianna said, "We have a girl!"

I was overjoyed. So that night, we landed at 01:10, our daughter was born at 01:15, and I arrived at the hospital at 01:20.

The look that Dianna gave me was a combination of looks. I later found out that she had been there all by herself. We had a friend Whitney, who was supposed to be there if I was going to be absent. As it turned out, Whitney's son had a fall and had to be hospitalized and she was not able to help out. I then understood that look. I got to name our daughter, and I chose Danielle Alexis Elder. A beautiful name for a beautiful little baby. Danielle almost didn't come into being, with so many difficulties during the pregnancy, but there she was a healthy baby girl. Unfortunately, I was not there when she breathed her first breath, but I did make it there minutes later. I gave Danielle the nickname of Snookums, or Snook for short, which is what I call her to this day.

My Chief put me on ground duties for over a month to ensure that I wasn't going to miss anything else. When I did go back to work, my first flight was a trip to somewhere in New York with the First Lady, Hillary Clinton, and Chelsea. When they saw me, they immediately asked about my new baby and wanted to see pictures. With it being such a short flight, I said I would show them the pictures on the return flight, and they agreed. Well, when they returned to the aircraft for the return flight back to Andrews, we all had forgotten about the photos.

After we landed at Andrews, I would always stand outside until the limousine would drive away just to ensure that they got off alright. The limo started and then stopped. I yelled up the stairs to look and see if they had left anything. As the doors of the limo opened, the First Lady said, "Jeff, we never saw any pictures of your new baby."

I was floored. But without hesitation, I ran upstairs and got the photos. And there we were: The First Lady, Chelsea and I on the tarmac of Andrews AFB looking at pictures of Danielle Alexis Elder. What a great memory.

About a week later, we received an envelope at home, addressed to Danielle Alexis Elder from President William Jefferson Clinton. In the letter, the President congratulated Danielle on her birth, both the First Lady and President later apologized that her father was not there on time for her birth because of his duties attending to them. Yet, something else special that Danielle can one day tell her children.

Space A Travel

Space A Travel is a lifesaver for many military families, and we used it many times. Once in 1999, Dianna, my two daughters and I boarded a C-5 Galaxy aircraft and flew from Dover AFB in Delaware to Ramstein, AB in Germany. In the middle of the flight, we hit some severe turbulence. It actually felt like that big aircraft was about to fall out of the sky. Thank goodness, only my wife and I were awake. I know my daughters would have been really scared. The flight lasted over eight hours.

Because I traveled so much with my job on Air Force One, when I got to travel with my family, I wanted them to enjoy something special. Normally a family trip to Europe would be very expensive. But the money I saved on airfare alone allowed me to put my family in the best hotels and give them a chance to know how it is when I travel around the world with the President. We utilized billeting while in the Kaiserslautern area, also known as K-Town.

On this trip we went to Germany, France, Austria and Luxembourg. Most of our time was spent in Berchtesgaden which is in the Bavarian Alps of Southern Germany. We stayed in a three-story chalet that featured an indoor pool and thanks to the manager, a full American Breakfast. This region is also known for some of the best foods and pastries in the world.

While in Berchtesgaden, I signed us up to attend a family dinner at a German Fest Hall. When we arrived for the dinner, they paired my family at a table with a German family. Prior to our trip to Germany, I spent a little time teaching my family simple German words. The German father at our table gave my youngest daughter Danielle who turned three on the trip some German bread, called Brotchen. Danielle in a shy voice replied, "Danke Schoen," which translates in English to "Thank you very much or thank you kindly."

All of a sudden, it was like the music stopped and everybody was looking. The Father whisked Danielle up and started dancing with her. They were so pleased to hear her at such a young age using their language. Needless to say, we had an outstanding time that night.

We also visited Sembach AB where I was first stationed when I lived in Germany. I even got to see some old friends and my old boss Calvin J. Allen, who is an American who now lives in Germany. That was outstanding. CJ or Allen, as we used to call him, took outstanding care of me when I was a very young troop and he kept me out of trouble. After all, 18 years old living in Germany, there is a lot of trouble that could have been gotten into.

I would spend much time with him and his family. We would often go to his wife's hometown of Beaver, near Trier Germany which to me is one of the most beautiful places in Germany. Because his wife was German, Allen spoke fluent German and he helped me learn. I was very grateful for the time that Allen and his family spent looking out for me.

Part Nine

September 11, 2001

September 11, 2001

Just about everyone old enough to remember September 11, 2001 can remember where they were when they first realized what was happening at the World Trade Center in New York. For me, I woke up in Sarasota, Florida as AF-1 had a one-night visit to the city. The flight attendants always arrived at the aircraft a minimum of two hours prior to take off to ensure that meals were prepared and sometimes crewmembers were fed. This started as just another normal day.

I was working as the Forward Galley Cook on this mission and I was in the galley when I first heard that a plane had flown into one of the World Trade Center buildings. The first thing that came to mind was, 'is it foggy up in New York?'

Many of the crewmembers went into the conference room to watch TV, which was tuned into the Today Show. Matt Lauer and Katie Couric were talking about a small commuter plane accident that had flown into one of the towers.

As we were watching, another aircraft flew into the other tower. At that moment, we all knew that this must be some sort of a terrorist incident and that our country was under attack. Col. Tillman summoned all crew members to the conference room and briefed us. No one was to call anybody or disclose anything about where we are. We all then went to our crew positions and prepared for an immediate takeoff.

When the President's motorcade arrived at the aircraft, I saw a show of security that I had never seen before. Usually Secret Service Agents had their weapons undercover but today everything was out in the open. Automatic weapons were out and ready for use. Everybody was researched prior to getting aboard AF-1.

I was watching as the President was coming up the stairs. There was no usual, stop at the top of the stairs and wave. He proceeded straight to the flying Oval Office. There were thoughts that the President or even AF-1 were also targets. AF-1 was being viewed as the "safest and most dangerous place in the world," at the same time.

Col. Tillman already had the right two engines running when the motorcade pulled up and when everybody was aboard, he fired up the other two and we were on the roll. We went straight to the runway, and there was the roar of those 747 engines, like never before. As we were jetting down the runway, everything on the plane was shaking.

We took off like a rocket and AF-1 was airborne in no time at all. Col. Tillman was flying that plane as if he had stolen it. Most of us breathed a sigh of relief as the safest place for us was in the air. At that point, we had no idea where we were going. Although President Bush wanted to return to Washington, DC, the Secret Service and other advisers warned against it.

Just minutes after we took off, the South World Trade Center Tower collapsed. Then about a half hour later, the North Tower fell. I will never forget the feeling I had, as a former fire fighter. I imagined all those people trying desperately to get out of those burning buildings as we saw the fire fighters rushing in to save lives. As a fire fighter, you always know that when the bells go off, there is a chance that your life might be the exchange for saving others. That is not something we dwell on, we just go about our job doing our best to save lives even at the cost of losing our own. Unfortunately, many of them never came out alive. This was one of the most heart-rendering moments in my life.

Information was coming in about a plane crashing into the Pentagon and another that crashed in Pennsylvania. It was then determined that the safest place for us was as far away from DC as possible.

At that point, Col. Tillman made the decision to fly around the Gulf of Mexico until other plans could be made. He took the aircraft up to 45,000 feet, which is the highest that we had ever flown, and I believe the limit for a 747. As I looked out the window, I noticed an F-16 Fighter Jet right off the wing. This F-16 looked so near us, that you could reach out and touch it. AF-1 had never had fighter jet escorts. The ironic part is the fighter jets were from President Bush's old Air National Guard (ANG) Unit—once the Ellington AFB, now Ellington Field.

Because we had intended, at the beginning of that day, to fly straight back to Andrews, the aircraft did not have a full fuel load. It was determined that we would land at an Air Force Base to refuel and put on food provisions. At 11:45 a.m., AF-1 landed at Barksdale, AFB in Louisiana. The plane was immediately surrounded by Air Force personnel wearing full combat gear with weapons drawn and ready.

The entire Base was on lock down. I guess it was to our advantage that Barksdale AFB was in the middle of their annual exercise called Global Guardian. The main purpose of this exercise is to test the military's command and control procedures in the event of nuclear warfare.

The President departed the aircraft to address the Nation on live TV. From this point on, only the inner circle of the President, Secret Service, a small contingent of Associated Press and AF-1 crewmembers were permitted to proceed aboard AF-1. I had the pleasure of telling any nonessential passengers and staffers to gather all their belongings because they would need to exit the aircraft before we departed. Our ground stop at Barksdale lasted one hour and fifty minutes.

The aircraft was filled with a full fuel load, additional water and food provisions. We were then all set to fly for an undetermined amount of time, and we did not know exactly where we were going. After all, this plane is capable of flying for days if needed.

After takeoff, the two F-16 Fighter Jet escorts joined us again. Col. Tillman made a decision to fly to Offutt AFB in Nebraska. This was another safe location and it had bunkers that the President could go in to communicate to his Cabinet and the world.

Upon landing at Offutt, it was again as if flying into a war zone as Airmen again surrounded us in full battle gear. We were not on the ground for two hours before we were airborne again. This time AF-1 was heading back to Andrews AFB, to get the President back to Washington. We had an impressive parade in the sky of escorts. There were F-15's above us, DC ANG F-16's on each wing, and the Texas ANG F-16's behind us. Eleven escort fighters in all.

Before we landed back at Andrews around 6:30 p.m., I looked out the windows and could see the smoke still coming out of the Pentagon. My first thought was for my friends I knew worked there. I was praying for their safety. Of course, Andrews was on total lockdown also.

As soon as the President was away from the aircraft, it was taken back to the AF-1 hangar. The AF-1 crew was told to leave immediately, because there was an aircraft in the air, and they did not know where it was going. The drive home was all a blur. I can only recall that when I pulled into my driveway, I sat there for a minute. All the events of the day were hitting me hard. I felt totally exhausted. The next thing I knew, my family came running out the front door crying and welcoming me home. My neighbors knew that I was a member of the AF-1 crew, and they too came running over to welcome me home.

When I turned on my phone, I thought it was going to blow up because I had so many messages from people from all over the world checking in on me to see if I was all right.

September 11, 2001, changed the world, as we knew it. The events of that day also brought our Country together and reinforced our patriotism.

The AF-1 crew is from the best of the best in the United States Air Force. On September 11, 2001, each crew position had a job to do. We are called the AF-1 Family, and on that day, the family came together and did an outstanding job taking care of the President of the United States of America and those who accompanied him. Job well done family.

The entire AF-1 crew for the mission on September 11, 2001, was given a Presidential Certificate in recognition of Distinguished Service which stated, "For your dedicated service to the White House and the Executive Office of the President following the attack on the United States of America." Signed by President George W. Bush.

In the days following 911, it was extremely eerie around my house. I lived in the air traffic pattern of Washington's Reagan National Airport. There were absolutely no aircrafts flying, and when flying opened back up, new No-Fly Zones were put up in the DC Area, changing air operations even more.

My Final Flight on the Big Plane

All good things must come to an end, and the time came for me to take my final flight, which we lovingly dubbed, "Finny Flight," on AF-1. My flight attendant crew was set, and it was mostly the gang of guys and gals that loved to hang out together. The trip was a four-day-three-night mission to Waco Texas and Salt Lake City Utah. Our first overnight was in Waco. It was fitting that I got the chance to visit Waco one last time as I had spent so much time there on missions with President Bush my last six years on the crew.

Those last few months flew by, and much of the time was spent remembering the amazing experiences I'd had. There were so many fond memories from those trips, like, playing racquetball with all the crew from Fort Hood, to having full access to Baylor University and finally those hot, hot days and nights when we spent the whole month of August there each year.

The citizens of Waco took outstanding care of the Air Force One crew. They loved their President and because we were taking care of him, they wanted to reciprocate. Most of the time, the crew would stay at the Courtyard by Marriott right next to Baylor University. The employees at the hotel would always treat us just like family members. We could always count on them to have a big cookout by the pool on those long stays. After all, Waco had become our home away from home. This finny flight allowed me to say goodbye to all of them and thank them for all the great memories. Thank you, Waco.

My last overnight would be in Salt Lake City. It was late in the evening when we arrived there, so it wasn't like we were going to paint the town red or anything like that. This was good because it gave me some time to reflect on my Air Force career. We had a nice dinner and then they toasted me one last time on the road.

I didn't get any sleep that night, so as I got up the morning of August 31, 2006, I prepared for my final takeoff and landing on this magnificent Boeing 747-200 series aircraft. Reggie and I were working the forward part of the plane, so it was business as usual - taking care of special requests and looking after the upper deck crew.

I took a little bit of time to walk to the rear of the aircraft and talk to our newest flight attendant, Orlando. I explained to O, as everybody called him, that I was passing on my torch to him. I went on to tell him that I was passed this torch when I first became a member of the AF-1 crew, and I was now continuing the tradition. It was now his duty to represent the Air Force and this crew to the best of his ability.

The flight seemed to go by so fast. Before I knew it, we were preparing for our landing at Andrews. Once we landed and pulled off the active runway, I made my final announcement to disarm the doors. It was at that point Reggie told me that President Bush wanted to see me. I went up to the Oval Office on AF-1 and President Bush thanked me for outstanding service and congratulated me on my retirement. We then took a photo to mark this event.

All of my crew members were congratulating me, and they gave me the Destination Card for going into Andrews, signed by many of my fellow flight attendants. Of course, my emotions were all over the place. I was both happy for this milestone but also sad that this was the last time I would be able to do something that I have truly loved doing. Flying on AF-1 was something that I loved, and I lived it to the fullest.

This would bring to a close my military flying career in which I massed nearly 6000 flying hours from a list of aircrafts to include the C-9C, C-17A, C-20B, C-20C, C-20H, C- 32A, C-37A, C-40B, C-141, C-137A/B, KC-10A and VC-25.

It is tradition that when you walk down the stairs on your last flight, your family is there to greet you and hose you down. True to form, there they were, and you know my daughters loved this opportunity. Getting their Daddy soaking wet while he was in his suit was priceless.

Retirement Ceremony

My official retirement ceremony was scheduled for Friday, October 6, 2006, just six weeks to do all the work in coordinating my farewell service. I wanted to make certain this would be an event that all would remember. With this being my special day, Colonel Tillman allowed me to do pretty much what I wanted to do.

I compiled an extensive list of invitees and had them sent out. Because the ceremony commences at the AF-1 complex, there are a lot of security issues that have to be attended to. I had friends and family coming from all over the United States.

I started looking through all of my old photos for a walk down memory lane of my career. I came across a letter from one of my old friends from Sembach, none other than the G-Man, Jerry Gallagor. I read the letter and at the end there was a phone number on it. This letter was over 23 years old, but I still called the number.

When a man answered, I told him that I had found this letter from a good friend that I was stationed in Germany with, and that I was trying to get in touch with him. I then asked if Jerry lived there and the man said, "No, but I am his father and I do know where he lives." I fell to the floor. I then asked if he could give my number to Jerry and the man replied, "You can give it to him yourself". With that he gave me Jerry's number.

I called the number immediately and to my surprise Jerry Gallagor answered. The first thing that I said to him was, "When I say Sembach, you say hoo." He then knew it was somebody that he played football with from Sembach. I told him that it was Woody as he used to call me. We both were so elated and talking so loudly that my wife came outside to see if I was alright. I had tears running down my face as I had just reconnected with an extremely good friend.

When I told Jerry that I was going to retire, he told me that he would be there for the event; and he was. I had so many people coming to town that I made several reservations at the Andrews billeting office and local hotels in the area. As for Jerry, he stayed with me at my house.

To my complete surprise, as Jerry and I were catching up, he told me that his wife was from Argentina and that she used to live in Paraguay. And when we met each other, we realized that we had met years before as she had worked the front desk of a hotel that I stayed in on a mission with then First Lady Hillary Clinton, to Paraguay. What a small world.

Finally, my retirement day was here. People were still arriving from out of town almost up to the time we had to go into the complex. I had over 200 people in attendance. Some of those included Ray one of our Elder racquetball players and a Pearl Harbor Survivor; Persi Arrington, who was a White House Press Pool member and former Harlem Globetrotter, and Geoff Peters, representing the USA Racquetball Board of Directors. I also had at least one person from each base that I had been stationed. From Sembach was Jerry Gallagor, Hancock Field and Homestead was

Nevador Evans and there were many friends there from Andrews.

When the ceremony started, Colonel Tillman and I were on AF-1. We then slowly walked down the stairs. When we got to the bottom of the stairs my family walked past us being escorted to their seats. Colonel Tillman and I then marched around and came up the red carpet. Just as we did an about face, the stair doors of the plane finished closing. At that point, my Niece LaToya Moore (her now-married name) came up to the microphone and sang the National Anthem. My cousin, Tommie Gregory Jr., presented the invocation.

It turned out to be an outstanding ceremony. When it was time for me to speak, I tried to make sure I thanked everyone, but of course my emotions were running so high that I forgot to mention a few—including my father.

After the ceremony, I was able to give one final tour as a member of the Presidential Crew to my family and friends. It seemed that everybody and their brother wanted to be included. All of the flight attendants were relocated throughout the aircraft as escorts and AF-1 Security was gracious in adding names to the list at the last minute.

After all of that, I had to quickly change out of my military uniform and get into my new suit and proceed to the Community Activities Center where I had my retirement party, and where we danced the night away to the sounds of DJ Chris. A great time was had by all except a few AF-1 members who had to leave early due to an AF-1 mission, early the next morning. It was a blessing that the plane and crew were in town long enough for me to have and enjoy my festivities.

My military decorations include the Meritorious Service Medal (2OLC), the Air Medal (1OLC), Aerial Achievement Medal (3OLC), the AF Commendation Medal (4OLC), Achievement Medal (2OLC), the Joint Meritorious Unit Award (4OLC), Armed Forces Expeditionary Medal (2OLC), and the AF Outstanding Unit Award (6OLC).

My Retirement Trip

My trip to California after I retired was a retirement gift to myself. It was very cost effective as I flew out utilizing Space Available flying. That is when a military aircraft is going someplace, they open space available seats to military, retired military, and dependents to fly for no cost. This is an excellent way to travel if you are not pressed for time.

The trip to California was to visit my Aunt, Uncle and cousins. My cousin Tony was very sick, and I wanted to go out and just spend some quality time with him. I am so glad that I did. We both had a wonderful time reminiscing about the wonderful times we had while growing up. The time that we spent in his hospital room is still with me to this day.

While I was in California, I received a call from one of my former coworkers. He asked me to send my resume because he was offered a job with Northrop Grumman at the Pentagon, but he already had another job that he wanted. I wasn't looking at the time, but I sent my resume anyway. The next day a representative from Northrop Grumman called me about an interview. I informed them that I was in California and when I would be home. They graciously set up the interview for when I would be home.

NGC at the Pentagon

I went to the interview after I arrived home. I felt as if the job was already mine. The first question they asked me was "Would you have any problems speaking to high ranking Generals?"

I replied, "I'm not sure if you saw my resume, but I have talked to the last three Presidents."

They said, "We know. We just had to ask." That was pretty much the interview and we started negotiation on the salary.

After being in the Air Force for over twenty-six years and then going to work for the Headquarters, Department of the Army (HQDA) was a huge change for me. New acronyms rank and just plain old jargon. But I was up to speed in no time at all. During my breaks, I would walk the Pentagon. In the year that I was there I walked the heels of five pairs of shoes as many of the Pentagon floors were cement or tile.

During lunchtime I was able to go down to the Pentagon Athletic Center (PAC) and play racquetball. Hold up, this was just like being back at Andrews on active duty. My sponsoring organization HQDA, even paid for my PAC membership. There was an Air Force Two Star General who loved playing me and he would have his aide call my office to set up playing times. My boss was ok with it as he put it, "We might need a favor and the General could help us out."

The women professional racquetball players were coming to town for a local tournament, led my Rhonda Rajsich the number one female professional player at the time and Shannon Feaster the Commissioner of the Woman's Professional Racquetball Organization (WPRO). I was able to coordinate for some of the ladies a tour of the Army Operations Center (AOC) and the Secretary of Defense's Office, where they signed racquets and gave away other racquetball equipment. Following the tour, the female players put on a racquetball demonstration in which Pentagon players were able to play the Pros. A great time was had by all, and it was special for me because also on the tour was Rhonda's dad, LT. Col. Retired, Dennis Rajsich who is no longer with us.

Federal Emergency Management Agency

I was at the Pentagon just over a year when the person that I had replaced, who was on military assignment down range, returned. I was given a raise and offered a position on a contract for the Federal Emergency Management Agency (FEMA), working out of Falls Church, Virginia. I didn't want to leave the Pentagon, but it was a done deal.

I was put on a team of Disaster Preparedness Specialist working for National Continuity Programs Operations, NCP/OPS. Working with FEMA gave me an excellent opportunity to learn about Continuity of Operations and Continuity of Government. I got to work on exercises all over the Country. This also allowed me access to many highly secret places.

This was a great job, but Northrop had two different contracts doing the same thing for the same office. It was inevitable that one would be eliminated at some point. And as it turned out, the contract that I was on, was the smaller of the two and we were eliminated in December of 2011. I was given a severance package and put on the unemployment line for a little more than a month.

Department of Homeland Security

I interviewed for several places, but I wound up taking a job in the Federal Government as a Tracker Watch Officer with the Department of Homeland Security (DHS). During my interview, I was asked if I could explain a situation where I was cool under pressure. I told them the story of where I was on September 11, 2001, and what our day entailed. A week later I was at the DHS New Hire Orientation.

I was now a Federal civilian employee working at the Nebraska Avenue Complex (NAC), in the National Operations Center (NOC).

As a Tracker watch Officer, I was responsible for tracking information from all events and preparing briefing materials for the DHS Secretary.

I enjoyed my job, however, it required me to work all shifts; days, swings and yes even the overnight midshift. I hated working mids. By then, I was a single parent of a 14- year-old daughter. I immediately upgraded my home security system at the displeasure of my daughter. I got motion sensors and cameras in and outside.

I enjoyed the work, but the work hours were not to my liking. Shortly after I started working at DHS, Bobby Clark from the Office of Emergency Management (OEM) at the Department of State (DOS) reached out to me inquiring if I was still interested in the Test, Training & Exercises Lead at State. When I told him I was, they put things in motion to make the move.

Of course, the leadership at DHS didn't want me to leave, but the move to State was a promotion and my team in the NOC even gave me a going away dinner prior to leaving.

This was a move that I very much needed for the obvious family reasons.

Department of State

When I first started at DOS in August of 2012, Hillary Clinton was the Secretary of State. It was almost like I was following her. After having been in the military for over 26 years and the working for FEMA, DHS and now DOS; I was acronym-ed out.

I also noticed a different culture working at the Department of State. I have always been the type of person that if you make eye contact with someone then you at least acknowledge them. That wasn't always the case here. But I would still try.

My first job was the Test, Training & Exercises Team Lead (TT&E). This position was a Monday through Friday, regular work hours. That made me extremely happy. My duties would include, developing plans, policies, procedures and capabilities to ensure the Department is prepared to respond to and recover from any emergency that may endanger its employees, information and property. I was also responsible for the emergency management exercise program for the Department of State.

Now I had to get used to some other things. The New OEM Director that was coming in around the same time as me, wanted to bring in his own TT&E Lead. This led to some problems because he made it obvious that he wanted somebody else in that position. I was intimidated at first, But that did not stop me from doing my job. I had a lot to learn about working at the State Department and I was all about learning everything that I could.

The first thing was learning about our manager's likes and dislikes. I saw a lot of tension between the two division directors, and both were at odds with the new overall director. It was like the three managers in the organization could never seem to get along with each other. None of the divisions were working together. That was not the best work environment, but I wasn't working shift work, so this was gravy.

The Department of State has a lot of formal training opportunities available, and I jumped right in taking some such as the Civil Service Orientation, Effective Speaking and Listening, Training and Presentation and other Leadership classes. I enrolled in the University of Maryland University College and completed my Bachelor of Science degree in Emergency Management. Then I followed up graduating from the Graduate School USA's Executive Leadership Program.

I became the Outreach Lead, and led a traveling team to

Department of State facilities domestically focused. Because of my extensive travel experience while in the military on AF-1, I was the ideal candidate for this position. Now, I was out front meeting people and letting them know how to stay safe at home and at work from all hazards. This is my passion. I love what I do and my team and I do it extremely well.

Working for the Department of State and the Office of Emergency Management in particular, has made me a much stronger and wiser person. Knowing when and how to use diplomacy is vital to the success of our mission. I also had the great opportunity to develop and author a new training program for all domestically focused Department of State employees called (PD-542 Emergency Preparedness Basics). It lets employees know how to stay safe both at home and at work.

Now, after nearly seven years at the Department of State, the time has come for me to move on. I am taking with me all of the good and bad things that I have learned here. I have met some really outstanding people, and met some that have tried to hold me down. To them I say, "You have only made me stronger and I thank you."

While I was in the military, I had some outstanding Level Five leaders who would always put the troops first. The Level Five Leader would do anything in their power to enhance the career of their subordinates, even to the point of losing them to someone else by promotion. Since then, in OEM, I have had managers that were all about themselves and only looking out for their friends or those in their circle. It's been a great learning experience.

My Life After Retirement

After going, going all my life, I could never have guessed that I'd one day enjoy doing something as simple as playing cards. Who thought I could sit long enough to play cards?

But, playing cards became a serious passion of mine as I slowed down from my years of playing racquetball. Not gambling, but just for fun and pride. My game of choice is Bid Whist. We call it the adult game of Spades. If you know how to play Spades, then you can learn how to play Bid Whist.

I first learned how to play Bid Whist when I was on a TDY to Egypt back in 1983 and fell in love with it. I, however, did not get to play very often, and I wasn't very good. That all changed when I went to the NCO Club at Andrews AFB. I found that there was a group of cards players that played all the time. When I say all the time that is exactly what I meant. It's like they lived to play cards.

The Club at Andrews was actually a very nice atmosphere. Think about It, you were in a place where you didn't have to worry about a fight breaking out, you had great music and food and you got to play the game you loved. For competitors, this was a dream come true.

The Club on Andrews, known at the time as "The Fox Den," was the best NCO club in the Air Mobility Command. People would come from as far away as McGuire AFB in New Jersey to visit the Fox Den.

There was always something going on, whether it was a famous name Comedy show, a famous singer, or special events like showing the Super Bowl, people came out to support. And the Fox Den took care of its members by member appreciation nights and special discounts for members.

If there was a Holiday in conjunction with a three-day weekend, we knew that the Fox Den would be having an All-Nighter. That was great for us card players. We would get to play cards all night in a safe environment. Who could ask for more?

Playing cards at Andrews allowed me to meet some really wonderful people who I am still very close to, to this day. Buddy, Cindee, and Six No Sam just to name a few.

Keeping Busy: Catering

Cooking had been a lifetime passion as well as a career for me. It wasn't as easy to walk away from it, as I would have thought. So yes... I ended up doing some catering on the side. Not only did Buddy Rowe and I play cards together but as I was nearing retirement, he invited me to come into the catering business with him. This is something we still do together, among other things.

Buddy was the head waiter for Helen's of Foxhall. This is a trade that he inherited from his Father Milton Rowe Sr. Mr. Rowe was also a waiter at the White House for many years. He had some outstanding contacts that he passed on to Buddy that we still use to this day.

Buddy had several great clients that we handled together, but one client would have us come over every Christmas Eve to work their family Christmas Party from 5 pm to 10 pm. That way, we would get home well before midnight.

This event was so much fun, and the entire family treated us as if we were family members. It got to the point that I couldn't see myself anywhere else on Christmas Eve.

When we were catering, it was like we were getting paid to have fun and socialize. Don't get me wrong, catering is very hard work, but we always managed to have a great time and get paid for doing it. It was a win-win situation.

The People Who Keep Me Sane

I want to say a special thank you to the people who are part of my life now, have seen me through some pretty hard times, but also laughed with me through some good times. Special thanks to…

Cindee

Cindee and I would often throw card parties at our homes. Anytime we were going to have people over for anything we would be sure to invite some card players and make the best of it. On one particular occasion, Cindee knew that it was my birthday, but we had just had a severe snowstorm and most roads were blocked for days. We all had cabin fever. Cindee called me to wish me a happy birthday, then when on the phone she said, "We should try to get together and play some cards." I immediately told her to include me.

After all, I had a Suburban which had 4-wheel drive and I needed to get out of the house.

Cindee also called her best friend Will, and we all met at her house. The snow was so deep that it took us some time to get into the driveway. But Will was getting out of his truck and slipped, disappearing in the snow. When he got up, we were all laughing so hard. That night was exactly what we all needed. Thank you, Cindee.

Six No Sam

So why do I call Sam "Six No Sam?" Because he is the one person who always thinks that he can get a six no, which is a very hard thing to do. Sam would start off with, "I tell you what I'm going to do." When we heard that we knew here comes a six no. He was actually pretty good at making it most of the time. Sam was always having many projects as he called them and movie making was one of them.

Movie with Sam "Red Carpet"

So, while playing cards with Sam, I made a comment. And the way I said it made him look at me and tell me that was what he was looking for in his new movie. I knew that Sam had done some work on films, but I had never seen any of them or participated in any. So, I guess my time had come.

Sam cast me in a starring role. I was to play a father whose daughter falls in love with an older man who turns out to be married and she gets pregnant. The story is all about what she does about it. The title of the film is A Tweet from Heaven.

Basileia Pictures Presents...

"*A Tweet From Heaven*"

A Samuel L. Goodson Production

Reserved Seating for Jeff Elder

It was filmed between Baltimore, Waldorf and the National Harbor—all in Maryland. Being a part of this production was very exciting. I had to get deep into the role to make the right emotions come out, and they did.

I had an outstanding time doing this project and it made me think for a little while that I wanted to continue acting or doing some commercials, but I never followed up on it.

However, I still keep in touch with my movie family. We communicate on most holidays.

Sam invited the entire crew to a Red Carpet Premier at the E Street Cinema in Washington DC. He set up us and our entourages to be picked up in stretch limousines and brought to the theater for a Red Carpet Event.

I got to walk the Red Carpet holding my Granddaughter, accompanied with those who meant the most to me. Along with my granddaughter, I had my mother Lula, my two daughters Brianna and Danielle and my girlfriend at the time, Vicki. This was a wonderful experience. You have to check out this short film. I'm sure you will get a few laughs and enjoy the tender moments of it.

Dolemite

Jeff and Vicki at Niagara Falls

I heard it said that man was not made to live alone, or at least that was my excuse when my friends asked why I was contemplating getting married again. At any rate, I had been alone in my home for a while as Snookums was away in college and figured it was time. Vicki, or Dolemite as I call her, is from West Seneca, on the other side of Buffalo.

We met some time ago and managed to keep in touch. Vicki had been a single parent to a wonderful son named Eric.

Eric and I were very close, and we looked at each other as a father son relationship. Dolemite always seemed to be the happiest when she had, as she called it, her two guys together. I would call her "Mother Hen," as she was always fussing over us in one way or another. Eric would love it when I took some of the heat off by telling Vicki, "Alright already Mother Hen." It would only last for a little while though.

Eric followed my career with excitement and anticipation. We talked about it often and he decided to also go into the Air Force.

He was to start off in the AF Reserves even though I wanted him to go into the regular AF. But Eric didn't want to leave his mom and grandma and with me being a mama's boy, I totally understood.

When the time came for Eric to enter the AF, I knew that it was going to be an extremely hard time for his mother and Gramma. He had never been away from home and I knew that Mother Hen would drive me crazy worrying about him. And she did.

Finally, the time for graduation had come. Dolemite and Eric's girlfriend Kristen made their way to San Antonio for his graduation. Unfortunately, this was a very busy time and my duties at the State Department would not allow me to attend. Eric graduated Basic Military Training with honors. He was scheduled to come back to start on-the-Job Training at the Niagara Falls Reserve Air Force Base. An additional technical training school was scheduled, but due to the federal government closing for funding; his training was cancelled and set for a later date.

We later found out that while at basic training, Eric managed to buy a motorcycle online and would get it when he got back home. Unfortunately, in May 2013, while Eric was out riding that cycle instead of being in his tech school (put off due to the government closure), he was involved in a horrible motorcycle accident. At only 21 years old, Eric was gone. When I got the call, I was devastated. If I was devastated, what do you think it did to my Dolemite? I knew I had to get up to New York right away to be with her.

I say that no parent should ever have to bury their child. But I don't make the rules. Only God knows the plan and when He calls, we all have to obey.

I told my Dolemite that I would take care of her; and that is what I intend to do. So, at our annual Fourth of July family celebration at my mother's house in Niagara Falls, I got down on one knee and in front of family and friends I asked Vicki if she would be my bride. There was a roar from the crowd and in between her tears, she said, "Yes!"

Vicki and I were Wed on July 18, 2015 at Beaver Island State Park, on Grand Island, NY. It was a beautiful, sunny day and I know that Eric was there with us. Of course, no wedding in the Niagara area is complete until you take photos in front of the Falls. The entire wedding party loaded into the Hummer Limo and headed to Niagara Falls for some of the most beautiful pictures ever.

My partner in crime and first cousin, Tommie married us. I was also fortunate to have my two daughters and granddaughter in the wedding. My best man was my long- time best friend Nevador, with Groomsmen Ice, Clint, Buddy, my nephew Robert, and Little Damon as my Ring Bearer.

During the reception I announced where we were actually going for our Honeymoon. You see, Vicki thought we were going to California only because I booked two round trip tickets on Southwest Airlines to California. I knew she could see it because I had to give her Rapid Rewards number. I stated that Sonoma Valley was only our first stop. I then told her we were off to Hawaii. Vicki screamed!

She had never been to Hawaii before, and I knew how much she wanted to go. Sonoma Valley in California, then we were off to Hawaii for a week and a half between Honolulu and Kauai. My Groomsmen Buddy and Clint played a big role in where we stayed and our interisland flying. Thanks guys!

In Honolulu, my good friend Joe Lee provided us with a convertible two-seater Mercedes to cruise and let our hair blow in the wind. Unfortunately, like a tourist I parked in the wrong spot and the car got towed. But Joe, being Joe was great about it. However, he will never let me forget about it. Thank you, my friend.

Marriage comes with life's ups and downs. To my wife I say, "I will do my best to take care of you for the rest of our lives. We will never forget precious Eric, but we must live our lives as he would have liked us to." We will keep his memory alive as our lives go on. Rest in peace Eric.

Laying a Wreath at Arlington National Cemetery

I have always said that being in the military and playing racquetball has helped me do some wonderful things and meet some of the best people in the world. One of those occasions came when the Military Racquetball Federation (MRF) came to the Washington DC area in 2016. This tournament was always scheduled near the September 11th commemoration.

As a part of this tournament, a few members were selected to dress in their service dress uniforms and lay a Wreath at the Tomb of the Unknown Soldier. I was asked, and of course I said yes, as I felt this was an extraordinary privilege. I just had to make sure that I could still fit into my uniform.

The three military members were Retired Army Colonel Conrad Morgan, Retired Navy Lt. Commander Steve Harper, who is one of the founding members of the MRF, and me. I have seen this done from a distance, but this was my first time actually participating.

First, it was great to just be able to fit into that uniform after 10 years of retirement. Next, I can't put into words the feelings I had when we were walking down those steps with all those people standing at attention, watching. If you have not done so, make it a point to attend a wreath laying ceremony at the Tomb of the

Unknown Soldier on your visit to Washington, DC.

My Coast to Coast Road Trip

I had never driven coast to coast before and when the opportunity arose, I jumped on it. I had missed an opportunity about ten years prior when my uncle and cousin did the trip. This time there was no way that I was missing out. My uncle Jeff, who lives in Alabama, and who I was named after, made plans to drive out to Phoenix..

The plan was to drive out from Dozier, Alabama to Phoenix, Arizona; pick up my Eldest Uncle, Willie and his wife and bring them back to Alabama to live. You see my uncle and his wife are all the way out there alone and needs somebody to look after them.

Well, things don't always work out the way you plan. My uncle's wife had second thoughts of moving back to Alabama and that stopped our plans. However, since we had already scheduled time to go, we decided to make the best of the trip anyway. The trip started off with me landing in Atlanta and meeting up with my Cousin Waverly. From there we set out for Dozier, Alabama. We arrived at my uncle's house at 2:30 a.m., transferred our bags into my uncle's SUV and we were off at around 3 a.m., with my uncle driving the first leg.

We were all excited about the trip, but my cousin and I were already tired from the drive from Atlanta. After all, I started that day off in Las Vegas, where I was best man in Ice's wedding, then flew to Atlanta and spent several hours with my daughter and new Grandson, then drove to Dozier Alabama. When we got in the car all I wanted was to get a minute of rest. But, that didn't happen right away. After all, we hadn't seen each other in a while and had to catch up. We then took turns - one driving, one navigating and one sleeping in the back seat. That was fine but it was that drive through Texas that put it on all of us. We went through the longest part of the state and it seemed that we were never going to get out of that state.

With three drivers, we drove straight through to Phoenix, arriving around 6 am on Tuesday. Of course, we had to wake up my aunt and uncle, but they were very pleased and surprised to see us. It was troubling for us to see my aunt and uncle, and knowing we would be leaving them here instead of heading back to Alabama where some family would be able to look out for them.

We only stayed there for about four hours, got breakfast and then got back on the road. Our next stop was Pasadena, California. This is where my uncle Jeff used to live and is where several of his children still reside. Many of which I have never met.

We arrived in Pasadena at around 7 p.m. The first thing that we did was get a hotel room, then we went out to visit family members and get a bite to eat. After several days of straight driving, it was great to finally get a nice bed to sleep in other than the hard seats of a moving car.

I also got to see my cousin Lynn, who now lives in Las Vegas. This is another of my uncle's kids, but we have known each other for many years. Lynn and I first met when I was still in the Air Force. He was in the Army, stationed at Fort Campbell in Kentucky and I was on the Air Force One Backup plane. My uncle gave me his number and I asked him if he would like to meet and get a tour of the plane. He agreed and asked if he could bring a friend. I said yes, and we started planning.

When the Air Force One Backup aircraft arrived for our ground stop, I notified Lynn and he came out to meet me. As soon as I saw him, I knew that we were related. I guess you can call it the Elder features. It was great to finally meet a cousin who I had corresponded with for many years but never met. Lynn told me that his best friend who accompanied him on the tour didn't believe he had a cousin that flew with the President, but when he saw me and I had the same name as Lynn's dad on my jacket, he finally believed it.

Back to the road trip. On Wednesday morning after enjoying that great night's sleep, we started with a wonderful breakfast at one of my uncle's favorite spots; then we were off to view the Rose Bowl. After several hours there, we said goodbye to my cousins and got back on the road heading back towards the East Coast.

Our first stop was Las Vegas. We only spent a couple hours there as none of us were big gamblers and for me, I was just in Sin City for six days for Ice's wedding the week prior. So, my meter was pegged.

We got back on the road and headed towards Flagstaff, Arizona. My uncle lived there years ago and still has many friends there that he wanted to see. We arrived around 8 pm. I was in a pair of short pants because it was hot in Pasadena and Las Vegas. But when I got out of the car in Flagstaff, it felt like winter. We quickly visited several homes until late in the evening.

When we got back on the road, we were going to drive straight through to Memphis, Tennessee. My cousin's brother lived there, and we were going to make a surprise visit. It was such a surprise that he wasn't even home.

But we found out where he was, and dropped in on his bowling league and spent a couple hours with him and his friends before getting back on the road to Dozier Alabama.

We arrived back to my uncle's house around 2 a.m. My cousin and I moved our bags from one vehicle to another, said goodbye to my uncle and started off to Atlanta. We both were tired but this last four hours would be nothing compared to what we all had just done.

We arrived back in the Atlanta area just in time for morning rush hour. Great! So that added a little time before we could get to Waverly's house. When we finally made it to his house it was such a good feeling to know that we had made such a long trip in such a short time, safely, and had an outstanding time enjoying each other's company. I can now mark driving cross country and back, off my bucket list.

The rest of that day was spent with just a little rest and as much time as I could get with my new Grandson. My daughter had a job orientation, so that gave me the opportunity to get some one on one time with Aiden. After that, we went out to one of my favorite BBQ joints, Fat Matts Rib Shack. I had not been there in over twenty years, but the great meals were still the same.

Unfortunately, in March of 2019, my Uncle's wife, who we had visited in Arizona, passed away on Wednesday evening. Then, my uncle passed away two nights later, at the same time in the evening. We attended a double funeral for them in Arizona. Rest in peace Auntie and Uncle.

Part Ten

Back to Where it All Began

Hello Again, Niagara Falls

When I first left Niagara Falls on August 1, 1980, I had no clue what the world would bring me. This journey has taken me to all 50 of the United States and all of the U.S. inhabited territories and allowed me to travel around the world several times over. I have been to six of the seven Continents, and one day I plan to go to Antarctica to complete all seven.

I have always said that the Air Force is a great place to start. It gives you the opportunity to grow up and they provide you with a trade. Although it's not for everybody, the military has educated me in far too many ways to mention.

From being 18 years old living in Germany, and traveling all over Europe, to being a member of the Sam Fox crews out of Andrews and traveling the world first class as a flight attendants, we were considered "professional tourists." We traveled the world First Class and got paid for doing it. Not bad, huh?

The perks and freedoms of being a member of the AF-1 crew are now gone, but long will live the wonderful memories of the people and wonderful friendships that I have acquired along this journey.

The Transition

I have served my country honorably with over 26 years in the military and 13 in the Federal workplace at places like the Pentagon, the Federal Emergency Management Agency, the Department of Homeland Security and the Department of State. I have been in places that most could only dream of.

Serving my Country in the United States Air Force was an honor that mere words cannot describe. The outstanding people that I have met during my military journey are a true testament to our hope in mankind. I have been truly blessed. To all of my Veteran brothers and sisters, I say "THANK YOU FOR YOUR SERVICE".

Now, I look forward to returning to my birthplace and home of Niagara Falls, where I love, and put in practice the things that I have learned while traveling all over the world and working for three different Presidents. Niagara Falls is still one of the most popular places to visit in the world, but for whatever reason the economy does not show it.

This was not a hard decision, because I always knew I wanted to come back home. So, the contacts I have made and the wisdom I have received, are going to be put to use. How? you might ask.

In politics you can't always pick the timing of your opportunities. When one comes your way, you have to seize it. I am entering politics because I think I can make a difference. I know I have to stand firm, without wavering, for what I believe.

I first ran for the office of Mayor of Niagara Falls because I was distressed about the continuing decline of our city and believed that I have the skills and connections to reverse that trend. Niagara Falls is a major tourist attraction which has been left in the dust with investments made elsewhere, neglecting the bright opportunities we can afford the region. I envision a Dynamic New Future for our city, using my national and international contacts to help fund and incentivize tourism.

And with that being said, Niagara Falls, New York, I was excited to run for Mayor and the opportunity to be a part of making needed change for our city.

After the race

My first time out in the political atmosphere was definitely a learning experience. In just a short amount of time we managed to garner nearly 18% of the vote.

We did our best with the very limited resources we had, but we fell short of our goal to be the mayor this time. So, we

congratulate the winners and wish them well. I am truly thankful to those who supported me, for without your help we would not have made it this far.

I remain committed to working for a Dynamic New Future for our great city and hope to find a way to deliver some of our proposals to life. We learned a lot over the past few months and met thousands of voters who are looking for a change and they will certainly get a change regardless of whether it is the one they wanted or not.

Tomorrow is another day, and we will weigh our options about the future. I hope the future is bright for our city and I will try to contribute to that goal. And speaking of goals; life is not worth living without goals. I am committed to the goals that I have set in my life.

Don't worry, Niagara Falls. I am not going anywhere, and you will definitely continue to hear from me. A Dynamic New Future is on the Horizon. What can or will you do to help?

Part Eleven

Memories

Family, Friends and Colleagues Share Memories

Cynthia D. Dunn, Bid Whist Card Buddy and Friend

I grew up in Lanham, Maryland. I've worked for the federal government for over 39 years, since 1980. While attending my first year at University of Maryland at College Park, I went to the unemployment office and a man by the name of Mr. John Plummer set up an interview for me with USDA under their Stay-in-School Program. I was selected for the program and began working there while I went to school.

After transferring to two other federal agencies, Department of the Amy and the Import/Export Bank of the U.S., I later transferred to the IRS, where I now work in senior management as a Business Unit Director for the Office of Equity, Diversity and Inclusion.

I met Jeff playing Bid Whist at Andrews AF Base. We latched onto each other because we were both trash talkers. Jeff LOVED to play cards. He had called me one day and said it was his birthday, and even though it was snowing he wished he could get the gang together to play cards. I told him, "Jeff, if you can get to my house we'll have a card party to celebrate your birthday."

And, that's exactly what we did.

One friend of ours fell three feet into a mound of snow, and we couldn't stop laughing.

Jeff's retirement took place inside the Air Force 1 hangar, and Jeff took us all on a tour of AF 1. People still don't believe that happened. Jeff is like a little brother to me. He is a very good friend. We still call each other periodically. I confide in him as friend.

One word I'd use to define Jeff is "committed." When he puts his mind to something, Jeff will see it through. He is also a committed friend.

Jeff's contributions to any organization would be his ability to communicate, to market what he believes in, and his infectious smile. Jeff is very well-rounded. He is both a company man and a family man. He does both very well. He called me when he became a granddad, and before I knew it, I was receiving all these baby photos. Jeff is a great dad. When he became a single father, he helped raise his daughters. He has such deep love and concern about his daughters. I think when he went through his divorce, I saw the fun, easy-going man transform into a much more serious father overnight.

Jeff would hold a Luau for his daughters' birthdays in his backyard, the whole thing… with leis, Hawaiian music, roasted pig, and dress. When planning for my father's 80th birthday, I wanted to have a roasted pig, and I immediately thought of Jeff. Not only did he send me the information as to where I can order the pig, but he called the owner to inform him that I would be ordering a pig and I am a friend of his. We've had lots of fun together. He's quite the dancer and loved to dance at the AF Base.

Jeff and I have a mutual friend, Sam Goodman, who produced a short film. He was looking for someone to play the father in the film. He picked Jeff to play the father and Anaiyah, my great niece, played his daughter. In the film, Sam had the father kissing his daughter on the lips, but Jeff insisted that it be changed because he did not want to kiss a young girl on her lips.

When Jeff retired from the military, I saw him become more structured. All the changes were for the better. I think Jeff's attributes that have been most beneficial was his communication skills and his resourcefulness. He's one of the most resourceful people I know.

Reginald Dickson

I was born and raised in Brooklyn. Jeff and I go back and forth about our hometowns – Brooklyn vs. Niagara Falls. I served in the Air Force along with Jeff beginning in September 1991. I was a student when I met Jeff. He was an instructor. When I cross trained to become a flight attendant, Jeff was already flying in the 99th Airlift Squadron.

Jeff and I flew AF I for a long time, and he gave his all to that role. But, at the same time, his family is everything to him – his wife, his children, his mother, his extended family.

Everyone knew Jeff was an avid racquet ball competitor. I played basketball. When Jeff wasn't off working somewhere, he was in the gym working out.

What is most memorable about Jeff is his charisma, and his love to laugh. Jeff and I reconnected over the last couple of years. I think he is finally able to sit still, but the one word I'd use to describe Jeff is "energetic!" He also uses his humor to make others feel more comfortable.

Jeff has lots of great qualities that have served him well over the years, again his energy has worked for him; his willingness to put a lot of effort into any challenge he has. He's a committed, devoted, trustworthy person who elicits confidence. A lot of his confidence has to do with his personal relationships. He also uses his humor to make others feel comfortable.

Jeff has always been very serious about his work. When he was my instructor, we were also friends. That didn't matter, he didn't let me slack on anything, ever. I recall that sometimes we would all be clowning around, but when something happened that demanded us to get serious, Jeff was the first to change to that serious military soldier.

He touched a lot of people in the military, it seems like I can never meet anyone who doesn't know him. He definitely deserves to have his story told. Everybody can pick Jeff out of a crowd because of his distinct laugh. He loves to laugh.

Jeff has remained the same person I first met—very grounded. As we all have, he's become more serious over the years, which to a great extent came with his career opportunities and educational advancement.

I'm not surprised Jeff decided to run for Mayor. He's always had a passion for community and public service. People may not understand it because he's so outgoing, but in his private time he's always found ways to help others. I used to call him "PR Man."

Briana Elder, Jeff's First Daughter

Ours was a military household, so Dad was gone quite a lot. When he was home, he was very strict, but he was always really cool. My parents moved around more before they started having kids.

My father taught us racquetball. It was a lot of fun, and a great family activity. He also taught us respect on the court. I played up until high school. We were all—Dad, my sister and me—nationally ranked at one time. I realized that I was more artsy, though. I was interested in singing in the choir and in photography.

My fondest memory. Growing up I had to wait until 16 to start dating or have a cell phone. Once I turned 16, my dad took me on a date to a really nice restaurant. Showed me how a lady should be treated. He told me that if a man didn't do everything that he did for me on that date, then he wasn't the one for me. Looking back, that's not only a fond memory, but something I have carried with me since then.

My family is a lot tighter knit than it used to be. Everything used to be on his shoulders. Since having my child, my father and I are much closer, though I live in New York, my sister is in Atlanta, and my father in Niagara Falls.

One word I'd use to describe my father is Determined. When he sets his sights on something, he goes for it with everything he has. Another word to describe him is "punctual." Punctuality has been instilled in me since birth. We would even have clocks in our house that were set ahead.

I would say my dad is most definitely a company man, but he also takes care of his family. I have great memories of family vacations, and we still go on family vacations together.

Transformation: I've seen Dad transform into a grandfather. It is so different to see him interact with my daughter from the way he was during my childhood.

The attributes I believe have been part of my Dad's persona since he was a child, are charisma—people really love him. I remember he was always the neighborhood driver.

I can't stress enough how much my dad cares about people, and his running for mayor is a good example of that.

Niagara Falls is very much a part of his family, too. I'm very excited to see him running for Mayor or any other office.

Jeff, Dianna and Their Girls

Danielle Elder, Jeff's Second Daughter

My father has always been a strong, protective and loving father. We always felt secure all through his time in the Air Force. We never doubted his love. He was at every event we had. We had a great support system.

If I got anything from my father, it was his strong competitiveness. He is also very strong-willed and doesn't let anything get in his way once he makes his mind up. We don't like to lose. My first sport was racquetball. there was a time when all of us—my dad and my sister and I were nationally ranked in racquetball. I don't play, now. In high school, I started getting involved in other sports.

What I remember from my childhood is a father who was very, very loving and loyal to his family. He puts his family first in every situation. He's not only a great dad, but a great granddad, too.

My relationship with my father has fluctuated over the years. When my parents divorced, I was a sophomore in high school, and

I moved with my father. We were very, very close. When we were around, he had to be a parent, so he sacrificed a lot for us. Now, that I am older, and a parent, I see and understand a lot. I appreciate even more what he sacrificed for us. Right now, I'm going through quite a lot and he is still there for me. Again, he's very, very family oriented.

My father has been all over the world and have had very diverse experiences. I've found that he has always been very adaptable. He's always very professional—especially in the area of punctuality. If you're on time, you're great. He has a great personality and is very much a people person.

He is both a company man and a family man. While he takes his company very seriously; since my grandmother got sick, he spends a lot of time in New York.

There are a couple of things that personifies who my Dad is. The first thing is when I was in labor, and at home having mild contractions. Dad was at work, so we sent him a group text letting him know I was in labor and on my way to the hospital. He texts back, "Don't go anywhere. I'll be right there to take you!"

The second thing was when I was in high school and my first boyfriend and I were going on a date to the movies. My father drove me to the movies to drop me off. We were sitting there waiting for my boyfriend's mother to drop him off and they were late getting there. My dad was so mad. He told my boyfriend that we were leaving, that it was unacceptable for him to be that late to meet me on our first date.

As for his run for Mayor of Niagara Falls, I'm very excited for him. This will be good for him. He knows what he has to do to get the city back to be the Honeymoon Capital of the World. And, his family and friends are there for him.

The transformation that's been most evident is his job from military to civilian. He has really progressed in his job. I've seen him under stress, but he finds ways to cope with it better, not let it fluster him as much. My father is a military man and he has that sternness about him, but I think becoming a grandparent has even changed that.

The attributes I believe have been with my father since he was very young are varied. One is professionalism. Even in high school, he didn't own jeans. I think the military instilled a lot of professionalism in him. Another attribute is personal appearance. That has always meant a lot to him.

He is extremely neat, and for him everything has its place. Time management is another strong attribute. I used to hate meeting my father because he had a habit of being early and structured. My Dad didn't believe in leaving home without making your bed. If you weren't 10 minutes early, you were late.

Uncle Jeff Elder

I'm 89 years old now. Jeffrey is my nephew. I still live in Dozier, AL where his mother and all his aunts and uncles were born. My family were sharecroppers. I left and went to New York when I was 18 years old and stayed there for six months before joining the military service and lived in Baltimore, Idaho, then Guam, Japan, and lived in Flagstaff, AZ for six years and Pasadena, CA for 10 years. I volunteered to return to Japan for three years. I started going out West after I retired from the military, but in 1975, I moved back to Dozier and have been right here since then.

In 1959 we packed up everyone—my mother and all her children—late one night and moved them from Dozier to Niagara Falls. Our oldest brother and sister were already there. We packed everyone up in there like sardines.

My brother, Jeffrey's uncle passed recently, so I'll go to Niagara Falls to visit Jeff's mother and our family. Jeffrey was really young when I was in Niagara Falls. It was a beautiful city then. Lots of people went to Niagara Falls from the south. It's changed a lot now. all the Plants closed, and now there are just the casino.

I drove to Birmingham the year Jeffrey was flying on AF 1 with the President, and they made a stop there. He set up a tour of AF 1 for me and some of my friends. If you add all jour years of service together, the Elder family has served over 100 years in the U.S. Military. I think it's great that Jeffrey ran for Mayor. I think he has a real chance especially with all the family and friends he has in the community.

One thing Jeffrey might not have told you is that all his uncles had nicknames: Boy Coolie, Biscuit and Son.

Mrs. Lula Elder, Jeff Elder's Mother

I was born in Dozier, Alabama and moved to Niagara Falls when I was 17 years old. That was exciting for me. My brother already lived here. He came down one year and brought most of us up to New York. I went to school in Niagara Falls. One brother still lives in Dozier I finished my schoolwork here in Niagara Falls. I never thought about moving back down south. I had all three of my children here.

I worked on the Air Force Base; then, for the Niagara Falls Memorial Medical Center for 16 years. I retired from there.

Jeffrey always got along with everyone and was always real outgoing. He was a friendly child and was a really a good athlete. He loved to play different sports.

When he was in grade school, the girls were carrying his books. Jeffrey and his cousin Tommy were really close. They'd sit in the middle of the floor in the living room and play different games. I would always get at him about the little girls carrying his books. He would just laugh.

Jeffrey is the baby. I have two girls who are older. When Jeffrey left for the military, we took him to the airport, and he was crying, and I was crying. I really hated to see him go.

He has always been outgoing, always got along with everyone and did well in school. When Jeffrey comes home just about everyone will come over to see him and he usually does a BBQ for them. Jeffrey is a great son. He treats me very special. He is very good to his family—his girls and his wife. I used to drive back and forth to Maryland regularly to visit him and his family.

Jeffrey and I have always been very close, and we still are. When he first went into the military, at Basic Training, I got worried because I wasn't hearing from him. I went to the Red Cross and told them I was worried something had happened to him. His First Sergeant, there, called him in.

Airman Elder said he was scared he'd done something wrong, but the First Sergeant told him I was worried something was wrong because I hadn't heard from him in a couple weeks. He made Jeffrey sit down right there and write me. And, he started writing me regularly after that.

I never would have thought Jeffrey would run for political office, but he's always been an outgoing person who wants to help his family and those around him live better.

Mrs. Vicki Fontaine Elder, Jeff's wife

Vicki and Jeff Elder

When Vicki Fontaine and Jeff Elder married in 2015 at Grand Island, New York's Beaver Island Beach, one might say their lives had come full circle. Though they never met during their youth, Vicki was raised in Cheektowaga, New York, less than 30 miles from Niagara Falls where Jeff was raised and where the couple met and eventually returned to follow Jeff's dream of becoming Mayor of his beloved hometown.

Vicki graduated from West Seneca East High School and earned her Associate Degree as a Certified Medical Assistant after her son Eric started kindergarten in West Seneca. Eric, who greatly looked up to Jeff and was highly impressed that Jeff flew on Air Force One, followed in Jeff's footsteps to serve in the United States Air Force. "We continue to miss Eric terribly since losing him in a tragic motorcycle accident in 2013 at the age of 21." She is so grateful to have had Jeff beside her this whole time.

Although it was his handsomeness that first caught her eye, she said with a laugh, it is his personal strength and giving nature that she admires and appreciates most. What started out as a genuine friendship, has become one of the most important relationships in her life; and "he knows I will always be his number one fan!" The one thing that many people might not realize about Jeff is that the real "Boss" in the family is a 4 pound furry white and black pup who adores the master chef in home.

Vicki readily admits to Jeff's phenomenal cooking! In addition to spending time with family and working in her chosen career field as a CMA in dermatology, she enjoys serving as treasurer on Jeff's campaigns. In fact, she enjoys all of the time she gets to spend with Jeff, who is notoriously dedicated to his work, and confessed that Jeff, her friend, husband, and life partner "still gives me butterflies."

Jeff and His Parents

Mr. Willie George Johnson, Jeffrey Elder's Father

I grew up in Greenville, Alabama; but I came to Niagara Falls when I was 17 years old. I'm 80 years old now. That's been a long time. I had a sister and brother already living here when I came. There is a lot of folks who came here from Alabama during that time. They came to find better jobs. Back in Alabama, the only thing they had was labor in the fields or working in the woods. I would go back to visit my family two or three times a year, until my mother died in the mid-eighties. I was there in June of this year for a family reunion, but I don't have any close relatives now. I have some distant cousins still there.

When I first moved to New York, I worked for a carwash, then went to work in construction for Local 91. My last job was with Airco-Speer Carbon-Graphite, a carving plant. I started out there as a laborer, then was promoted to train operator. It was a nasty job, but it paid really well. I retired from there after 37 years.

I met Lula Elder here in Niagara Falls, not long after I moved here. She was from Dozier, Alabama, but I didn't

know her when I lived in Alabama. Jeffrey was born in 1962. Even though we never married, we've remained friends over the years, and we both feel very lucky to have Jeffrey as a son.

Niagara Falls has seen a lot of changes since I moved here. I married and had three children. Jeffrey is my oldest child. My wife, Annie, fell in love with Jeffrey after she got to know him. He was the first person she sent an invitation to, when she retired from her job. She passed several years ago.

Jeffrey is a person that everyone loves. He has the gift of gab and he never meets a stranger. He loves his family and whenever anyone needs him, he is always there. As a father, I'm so proud of all my children. Not one of them have ever given me any trouble. I've never had to get one of them out of any trouble. That's something to be proud of.

I'm really surprised that Jeffrey decided to run for mayor, even though I heard him talk about it. I'm very proud of him too. I know he will make a good mayor for this city.

Unfortunately, I've had some health problems and can't get around like I used to and can't help him like I'd like to, but thankfully, he has his sisters and family to help.

The words that best describe Jeffrey are "just a nice guy." He has made us all so proud of him, and he seems to get better every year. He hasn't changed so much from when he was a child. I think when he was little, I expected Jeffrey to grow up to be the person he did, a wonderful young man.

I guess the thing that I remember most about his childhood is his roller-skating. He was known all over for his roller- skating. The guys would come to me and tell me how good he was, and I'd say, "Where you think he gets it from?" Of course, I never could roller-skate, and I don't think his mother could either. I think it was just something he

decided to teach himself. I still see people who used to roller-skate with him, and they'll still talk about how good Jeffrey was.

I also remember that when Jeffrey came home on leave for the first time, my car had broken down and I was a little scared to ask my wife if he could use her car; but when I did she was already about to tell me Jeffrey could drive her car and just bring it back when he finished up.

His mama and me were both happy and sad to see Jeffrey go into the military. He went in right out of high school and was there for over 26 years. He made us all so proud. I never went into the military, but Jeffrey had several uncles who did, and he always wanted to be like them.

Willie Elder (Jeff's uncle)

I'm Jeffrey's uncle. His mother is my sister. I went right into the Air Force after high school I stayed there for 30 years. Like Jeffrey, I was first, a fire fighter, and then worked as a crew member on an airplane. It was a great experience, and I flew all over the world.

We grew up in Dozier, Alabama, but most of my siblings and I migrated to Niagara Falls in the early 1950's. Most people in the community left Alabama around that time and a lot of them ended up in New York. My Aunt and Uncle went there first, then we followed. Most of us moved to either Buffalo or Niagara. I distinctly remember when my three older brothers left home to go to NY.

We had to walk to school. It was nineteen miles, but we passed two white schools to get to our school. In 1959, my oldest brother was in the Air Force, and he drove down to Dozier and picked up the whole family. We left in the middle of the night. I was in my early teens, in high school.

We moved to Niagara and I finished high school there.

It wasn't such a stark difference because we didn't move into town. We lived outside the city, in the county. It was a big community of families and children. There weren't the problems associated with urban New York.

Back then, there were lots of steel mills and chemical plants. Plenty of good paying jobs. Since then, most of those mills and factories have closed. Everything changed. Even the farms back in Dozier changed. No one can live off farm labor anymore.

When Jeffrey was little, he had a cousin and the two of them were always running around together. They were the first ones to show up on their bicycles in the morning. I was always close to Jeffrey, though I was gone most of his childhood. I'd see them during the summers. After I got married and had a couple of kids, Jeffrey seemed to always be at our house. He'd come when school was out and stay two weeks at a time.

I retired from the military at Travis AF Base located in Solano

County, halfway between Sacramento and San Francisco, California.

After Jeffrey graduated from High School, he went right into the Air Force. He had the same jobs as I did during my military career—firefighter then flyer. He was also a competitive athlete. I was an athlete throughout my career, and still do senior sports—softball and officiates competitive sports. Jeffrey always said he was encouraged to join the military by what he saw me doing.

Jeffrey hasn't changed much at all through the years. He's always had some pretty special traits: friendly and outgoing. He doesn't meet a stranger, and he's always ready to help. He always wants to be involved…and, at the same time, he always could find a way to demand attention. Back

in the day when nobody in his community was roller- skating, Jeffrey taught himself to roller-skate and could outdo just about anyone doing it. Nobody could believe how good he was at that, just teaching himself.

Jeffrey was the kind of person that he was always there at those special times. He would always show up during those special moments in my life—weddings, retirement and moves. It was so ironic that I ended up going to his retirement in 2006. One memory that will always be with me, is how, when my son died, Jeffrey was right there to support us, and made it clear to us that we still had a son.

Jeffrey always gives 100% to whatever he's doing. If he doesn't know something, he'll learn it because he always wants to be the best. Maybe he got some of that from me. I always tried to instill in young people that they shouldn't be satisfied with the status quo; whatever it takes always give it your very best.

Mrs. Vivian Elder (Jeffrey's aunt)

I remember Jeffrey spending his summers with us. We enjoyed having him, loved him dearly. It was so wonderful watching him grow up.

We're very excited about him running for Mayor. He's taking on a big plate, but the city needs him, and he wants to help and give back to his city.

Jeffrey has always been such a loving, kind and respectful young man.

Richard Eisemann, Military Colleague and Friend

I'm from Georgia. I graduated from high school at 18 and entered the military at 21. I traveled all over Europe, and to

Korea. Jeff and my paths crossed in the early 90's, through

racquetball. We were both competing in the Air Force Racquetball Tournament. We bonded immediately and played doubles. We always competed together, but, I was the better player. We ended up as family. I retired in 2000 after twenty years in the military. After retirement, I went to Ireland to play in the Irish Open Racquetball tournament with Jeff.

Jeff has an outgoing personality, and always somehow ends up the center of attention. He was always very approachable. He's great with a group of people. We could tell each other just about anything. Mainly it was always about our love of sports that we bonded around. We just really related to each other.

The one word I think describes Jeff best is "engaging." He is approachable, welcoming, passionate about whatever he's into, including his work on Air Force 1.

Jeff's contribution to any organization is his accountability and integrity. He was always dedicated to his job, and never worked "on the clock." He was there as long as he needed to be, to get the job done.

I would say Jeff is a company man. There's a balance, but his call to serve took precedence over anything else, though he definitely loved his family.

I can't say Jeff changed a lot in the 25+ years we've known each other. I know we all learn from our early years, look back and say we wish we'd done things a little differently. I did see Jeff grow out of being a military man into a civilian, and now into politics. I guess he's still growing.

If there were two attributes about Jeff that I think has been with him since childhood, it would be his outgoing personality and his passion for life. People seem to always

gravitate toward Jeff. I guess it's because he always seems to be the life of the party. Then, on the other side he is always helping someone.

Mike Evans, Friend and Military Colleague

Jeff is "the brother from another mother." We have a lot in common, not the least being we are both proud New Yorkers. Jeff was born in Niagara Falls in a community dubbed The Love Canal, I was born in Pennsylvania, but moved with my parents to Buffalo—just 20 miles from Niagara Falls, at a very young age. Jeff's family, much like mine, were blue collar workers. My father eventually became a civil servant in the Department of Health in Buffalo.

Mine and Jeff's high school football teams often played against each other. Our paths didn't cross at that time, but less than a decade later we both chose the military, and we both ended up in the Air Force. Like me, Jeff went off to the military immediately after high school. I also trained at the Vocational Education school's food preparation course during high school.

In 1980, I was stationed at Andrews AFB, and started out at the 89th Airlift Wing, where I was an attendant and instructor. By 1989 these two New Yorkers were flying together on the C9. My first interactions with Jeff was, as his instructor evaluating his writeup, on how well he did on the trip. I was often prone to pranks, so I created a bogus evaluation for Jeff, telling him he had scored really low, and his procedures were subpar. When I saw the look on Jeff's face, I laughed and told him it was a joke and that he actually did a great job.

I was selected by the crew of Air Force 1 in September

1989, and specifically by Colonel Robert Barr to join the Air

Force 1 crew. The first time I saw a 26000 Aircraft was on television in 1963 when the plane carried President Kennedy back to DC after his assassination. I was just five years old and only knew that the President was the richest man in America.

Coming on the AF 1 crew is based on a selection process by the chief pilot of the plane and fellow crew members of AF 1, with the final decision by the AF pilot. Names were placed into a hat for selection. I ended up participating in Jeff's selection for the AF1 crew.

In 1985, I lived on the Andrews AF Base, and was able to watch the hangar and air lift being built for the first AF1 and backup—28000 and 29000 airplanes. Those planes are still in service today and are expected to be retired in 2022 or 2023. Jeff and I worked together over four years, though we didn't always fly together.

Our Air Force 1 flights took us around the world. Most memorable, was a trip to London with President Bush in 1991 for an economic summit. while the official business took place, the 54 crewmen plotted out space in Hyde Park and held a baseball game with hundreds of English onlookers. While we didn't fly together all the time, we'd run into each other in the gym where Jeff was recognized as an outstanding racquet ball player—one of the top ten players in the state and in the top 10 percentile in the Air Force.

One of my most memorable flights was in 1993 with Mrs. Clinton during a three-city tour in New York. When we flew over Buffalo, there was a snowstorm. Mrs. Clinton told her assistants that she knew she had an appointment in Syracuse, but she wanted to make time to meet the crews' families who lived in the city. She took half an hour meeting our families in freezing weather. Both Jeff and my families were proud to meet Mrs. Clinton. They would also get to meet President Clinton in 1996.

Another proud moment was when my Godmother, friend and former boss Lorraine Goszewski, owner of the Heritage Inn Restaurant in Buffalo, was able to cater three meals during flights with Mrs. Clinton, and one meal during President Clinton's campaign tour that included a stop in Buffalo.

President Clinton and Jeff in Buffalo, NY

During one trip, Lorraine invited the entire airplane crew to her restaurant for dinner.

Lorraine gave me my first job as a pot and pan dishwasher and short order cook, where a made a whopping $1.65 per hour.

Jeff Elder was always positive, with one of the biggest laughs of anyone I know. His most outstanding traits are his professionalism, integrity, trust and loyalty. He is a family man and I was happy Jeff was part of our "family" aboard AF 1. Those were relationships I'll never get to repeat, but I'm so grateful for those opportunities. We had a tight-knit group. I think we wrote the blueprint for the AF1 crews who came behind us.

Jeff and I were closer than I am to some of my own family. We went through so much together. We were truly kindred spirits. One of the first things I noticed about Jeff was that he would always say a quiet prayer before each meal, and I always respected that very much.

I retired in 1999, as Superintendent of AF 1 Kitchen, which was a 3000 square foot kitchen where the crew prepped, stored and prepared meals for the President of the United States of America. Another memory: Jeff was invited to participate in a National Geographic documentary, and I assisted with the iconic photograph of Air Force 1 flying over Mt. Rushmore.

Jeff and I had lunch in June 2019, in Niagara Falls. It was the first time he'd met my youngest son, and he told me about his race for mayor. He even gave me one of his Jeff Elder for Mayor campaign flyers.

Nevador Evans, Friend

I'm retired military, from North Carolina. I was drafted into the Army after four years of college. Though I was drafted by the Army, I opted to join the Air Force instead. I was not looking forward to going over their sweating tears and unknown causes for an unpopular war. Early into my military career, I applied for Officer Training School (OTS) which allowed me to become a commissioned officer. My first assignment was at Myrtle Beach Air Force Base, South Carolina, I remained there for three years working in the transportation career field.

I first met Jeff in early 1983, while stationed at Hancock Field in Syracuse, New York. We were both stationed there as part of the group who would assist in base closure. We became very close friends forever.

Jeff was an avid racquetball player and I was one of the few people who were able to win a game and talk about it. I don't think he ever got over that, but our friendship lasts to this date. Jeff traveled around the world and won all kinds of tournaments as a premier representative of the Air Force.

We were stationed together later at Homestead Air Force Base Florida. Afterward, we always stayed in touch. Our relationship has truly been rewarding over the years and continues to this day. I'd say, Jeff is like a biological brother. We'd always have Christmas events at our house and invite Jeff and his beautiful family. What I remember most about Jeff is his high energy. He was always doing something, and he had a big heart. If you needed something done, he was always there to give a helping hand. He was and is a strong believer in doing the right thing for all of mankind. He's the real deal without questions.

My one-word description of Jeff is "charismatic." He really connects to peoples' concerns. Most of the time you don't even have to ask Jeff twice, he just kind of knows what is needed. I have to say I've never met anyone like him. He is likeable and is a good listener.

Jeff has always been a go-getter. He won't refuse any challenge.

He's dependable, and a great listener who considers everyone's side before making a decision or offering advice.

Jeff is both a company man and a family man. He is a perfect balance of both. He really loves his family... sticks with them like glue. I've never seen a man who loves his mother so much. I know she's very proud of him. He takes his work very seriously, and sometimes I wonder how he gets it all done.

One story that I recall with Jeff is during the time we were both stationed at Florida Homestead Air Force Base. In college, I majored in Vocational Industrial Education (mechanical field) and I've always been a car buff— collecting, restoring and repairing cars. I had an old '58 Volkswagen at the time, and Jeff really loved that car. He told me one day that he was going to find him an old car that I could restore. He went somewhere and came back with a Mustang that didn't have a hood on it. I had to tell him I couldn't restore a car without a hood. Later on, after I moved to Hampton, he brought another Mustang down for me to work on a 1966 convertible Mustang (with all component parts) that I was able to restore for him. Jeff still drives that car, and it still looks great.

I would have to say Jeff hasn't changed in the 38 years I've known him. We're both a little bit older, but he's still the mild-mannered person who is always willing to go to whatever lengths it takes to get things done. He is the type of person who wants to be all he can be and assist others in need. Believe it or not, I've never heard Jeff utter a curse word. He jokes a lot, but they're clean jokes.

There's nothing I wouldn't do for Jeff because I know he feels the same way about me as well as others he'll represent. I was so proud when he went back and got his degree after he retired. I wish him the very best in the pursuit of all challenges he may face in life. I was informed that he is facing political challenges and wish him well in that pursuit. I'm not surprised, but I can definitely see him in that role as a people-person. He has the personality, drive, and ambition to make a difference.

Gerald Gallagher, "Brother from another Mother"

I met Jeff in Germany, and we hit it off right away. We played football together and traveled together to Switzerland and Paris. I was in Germany for two years, and we played racquetball together. He used to kick my butt, but we would play all over Germany.

Jeff and I lost contact for 20 plus years. During that time, I moved to Tulsa and went to work for American Airlines. One day I was out in my yard working on my car, and he called me out of the clear, blue sky. He said he was getting ready to retire from the military and was going through his numbers and found my old number. It was my dad's number in Pittsburgh. He called my dad first, and dad gave him my number.

After we reconnected, I received this big, elaborate invitation. Jeff invited me to his retirement. I went, and my wife and I stayed at Jeff's home. I found out he had worked on Air Force 1 for the last part of his tour with the military. One of the greatest moments was Jeff giving us a tour of AF 1. Since then, we've stayed in touch.

Never in a million years would I have thought Jeff would write a book. He told me of his new political adventure. He promised me if he wins, he'll have a big party. I will surely be there.

Jeff is outgoing, funny. In all the years I've known him, I never saw Jeff "down," or mad… unless we were playing football and we were competing. We could be pretty fierce. My one-word description of Jeff: A great human being. Jeff is down to earth, and happy-go-lucky. Jeff's strengths: he's a great leader, a go-getter who will always find a way to get what he goes after. Jeff is a great family man. He did lots with his kids, was always there for them. he could be a company man, too. He was a fireman when we first met, then switched to work on AF 1.

I don't see any change in Jeff over the years. When I saw him for the first time in over 20 years, he was the very same person. Jeff is an outgoing person, and I think he will make a great Mayor. We had some good times, especially the times we'd go off on own to explore the places we were in. When we met, no one could believe I was so fast for a white guy. I raced a few times and beat everyone. Both Jeff and I were very competitive. We used to go at each other, but always having a great time.

Samuel Goodson, Friend, Military Colleague & Card Buddy

I'm originally from Houston. My wife was military too, so we moved to the East Coast onto Andrews AF Base, after 9-11. We met Jeff and his family in early 2002, and soon became good friends.

I've written several screen plays, but just one film, *A Tweet from Heaven*, a short film that was a 15-year process. It was something I had a passion for but couldn't afford to do fulltime. I'd been working in the film industry for many years, and I also do stage plays. One of those plays was *A Text from God*.

I started developing *A Tweet from Heaven*. I had played the father in the stage play, but when I started producing the film, I needed someone to cast as the father. I looked for people who fit the profile. It turned out that Jeff was a natural. He had the personality of the character. When I asked him, he told me he'd never acted before, but I convinced him he naturally had the profile we were looking for. That's how he came to be in that role.

Jeff did a lot of work to get ready for the role. I have never known

Jeff to be irritated or mad. He always has a smile on his face, but there were a couple of scenes where he had to be angry, and I had to work with Jeff to get him to the point where he could be mad and upset. I tutored him and finally, he was able to pull it off. We had a wonderful time doing the film.

That was the first hallmark of our relationship. Secondly, when Jeff had his retirement party, he invited my wife and me. It was in the AF 1 Hangar. I had to go through layers of security, but it was all worth it. That was the highlight of our lives. I got to tour Air Force 1. That really was exciting. I told Jeff, "I need to hang out with you, more often."

Jeff and I are still good friends. We used to play cards together, but my wife and I moved to Waldorf, and aren't able to do the card games anymore. But we remain close. He's one of those people who will always put you on the list if there's any kind of event he's doing.

My one word to describe Jeff Elder, is "inspirational." His strengths are his ability to work with people and bring cohesiveness to a group. He has strong people skills. Jeff is more a family man than a company man. His family always comes first. I've known Jeff since 2002, and he hasn't changed. The main thing about him is the way he values family. I know his mother way before we did the film. I knew him before he had the granddaughter. Now, he's beginning to realize the importance of his legacy. He has even a stronger tie to his family, now.

As for the attributes that have been with Jeff since childhood, I believe a lot of how Jeff is because of his mother. I look at their relationship and have to conclude that a lot of who he is can be accredited to her.

As for Jeff's mayoral run…I never really pictured Jeff going into politics, but when he started talking about it, I saw it. It's all about helping others, doing for others. I think it's a good move for him. I will be an advocate and supporter in whatever he does. I think he will be good for the community.

Don Humpheys, Friend & Military Colleague

I first met Jeff in 1996. It was during the reelection campaign year for Bill Clinton and Al Gore.

VP Gore with the Elder Family in Buffalo

The first thing I remember about Jeff is his smile and laughter. We were at the President's hangar. Everyone was professional, but we had some characters, too. I remember we gave everyone nicknames.

I was invited "by invitation only," to come over and join the crew for flights with the first lady. I thought I had a great interview. I was a bartender, so I wore a tuxedo to the interview. Jeff gave me the nickname of "Blender," because I had a special kit in my bag that I took with me everywhere, including overseas. I worked for a while as a bartender in the jazz clubs in Turkey.

Ironically, both Jeff and I knew how to roller-skate and would end up competing. When we went to some of the preppy schools, I'd show him some of my roller- skating moves. While I held my own in roller-skating, I could never compete with Jeff in racquetball. One day he invited me to play with him, and when I told some of my colleagues who I was going to play, they all just shook their heads and said, "Good luck." It was later that I realized just how good Jeff was.

Jeff and I still have a close relationship. We try to get together about once a month. If we're both in town, we'll meet for lunch. Our friend Randy Tusing used to do a Memorial Day barbecue. Jeff would come down for that. Basically, it was a block party where neighbors would chip in for food and drinks. Whoever was in town was welcomed.

When you work on the jet and travel all over the world together, you bond pretty quickly. Air Force 1 was our home away from home. Those guys have been my family. We were called S.A.M.— Special Air Mission/Sam Fox. We still have our S.A.M. Fox Reunions every three years.

Some of our Supervisors flew with five Presidents. There is a tour at the National Harbor that offers visitors a reenactment of the AFI experience that includes a video tour of AF I narrated by former AF I pilots who share information about Presidential transportation all the way back to George Washington. When one of the 747 Cargo jets was retired, they placed it on the harbor, and now visitors can see, close up, a replication of the AF I cabin. The project is funded by donations, including the Secret Service. If I had to describe Jeff in one word, it would be "passionate"—with everything. He's also enthusiastic. he brings solutions to challenges and advocates for success every time. His thing is to get it done safely and effectively, always. Jeff would always stay 1-2 steps ahead of the itinerary. He was a great mentor.

While some might say Jeff had a domineering personality, the most important thing was that he wanted everyone to succeed. I used to go to some of his family reunions. He would always make sure his family knew where he was, and that he was safe; and he always let them know when he made it back.

On small jets, we started with a small crew who were responsible for making sure that the trips were successful for 18 days. If you can handle that by yourself, you can handle AF I. Students have returned from those trips, and they'll say, "Thanks, Jeff, for teaching me." That's how that bond is built.

I'll never forget when Jeff met my dad, he said, "Don Sr., I know the apple didn't fall far from the tree… it's been such a pleasure to fly with your son." Jeff was definitely a family man. He loved his family even though our jobs took us away from them a lot. We ate a lot of chicken wings watching the Superbowl in our rooms In faraway places!

Transformations? Jeff has grown and matured over the years. His competitiveness is still there, but he realizes he's gotten a little bit older. I'm super excited about Jeff running for Mayor. That would be something really cool. I can definitely see him doing it and doing it very well. There's always going to be positives and negatives to public service and politics. It can be a double-edged sword, but I know Jeff and he'll keep it all close to his heart.

Clint Imholte, Friend & Military Colleague

Jeff and I met through racquetball at Fort Sam Houston in San Antonio, Texas in 1998. I was on the Army Racquetball Team and

Jeff was on the Air Force Racquetball Team. Jeff was a fierce competitor, and you could see his passion for racquetball. He wasn't the most gifted player on the Air Force team, but he had the heart of a lion. We knew every match with Jeff was going to be a battle and that he was going to dive in multiple rallies and never give up on any shot. His passion for the game and his competitiveness drew many admirers.

Jeff and I met routinely at the Interservice championships thru the years and became good friends. In 2001, Jeff was selected as the Captain of the Air Force team. He wasn't the senior player on the team, but he was selected because of his ability to bring the team together. Although racquetball is an individual sport, Jeff created a culture on the Air Force team that moved from a "me" to a "we". It is the only year that the Air Force team beat the Army at Interservice, and I credit that win directly to Jeff's leadership.

Jeff had always been a leader and it didn't surprise me that he was elected as the Military Representative for the United States Racquetball Association (USRA) in 2002. He served the USRA for eight years. Jeff always pursued roles of responsibility or leadership. He energized racquetball within the military and was solely responsible for keeping racquetball as an interservice sport. Jeff's passion for the game didn't stop in the military, he brought his passion to his family and his girls were excellent racquetball players.

While racquetball was the vehicle, Jeff was the force keeping us all together. I was living in Hawaii and Jeff visited via Air Force One. We were able to pull together all of the racquetball players in Hawaii to play in a one day shoot out. Afterwards, we all congregated at my house and enjoyed food and family. Again, Jeff brought inclusivity to the sport.

Over the years, I had many discussions with Jeff about life on Air

Force One. I knew that selection to serve on Air Force One was a very competitive process and that everyone on that crew had to be at the top of their specific job specialty. He shared many stories of his relationships with some of the most powerful men in the world. He had a unique insight into the world of leadership and politics at the highest level. The lessons learned and the leadership experiences on Air Force One were priceless for Jeff. I always appreciated Jeff sharing stories and Presidential items with my family. Just another way Jeff brought us all together.

It's clear to see that Jeff's upbringing, leadership, responsibility and experience on Air Force One are what propelled him to success. While a charismatic leader, he has a sense of humor that can make light of any difficult situation. I always appreciated his ability to talk to anyone about anything. Jeff never met a person that he didn't call a friend. What I most admired was his ability to stay loyal to those not present. He never bad-mouthed other people which seems common in today's world. He always treated people as if they were present and focused on the positives rather than the negative.

When Jeff retired in 2006, we continued to stay in touch over the years. Jeff shared with me his vision to be the Mayor of Niagara Falls. Not because it is a high paying job… But more so because he felt the city had been neglected and that he could bring leadership to renew and energize the city. My family and I attended his wedding in July 2015 in Niagara Falls.

Throughout the years I have known him, Jeff always had a demanding job with exceptional levels of responsibility which required extensive travel. But Jeff never put his family on the back burner. Jeff was both a family man and a company man. He always managed to maintain a great work-life balance despite the job he held. Like racquetball, he loved his family with a passion.

My family and I are proud to call Jeff our friend. He is a man of character, faith, family and a desire to help others succeed. Jeff always had high standards for himself and his work. In my humble opinion, Niagara Falls would be very fortunate to call Jeff their Mayor. His leadership. inclusivity, and altruistic character will take the city to the next level.

Thank you for asking me to contribute to your memoir. I appreciate and respect you and our friendship. May God continue to bless you and your family.

~ Clint, Dawn, Clint Jr, Nick, Jesse, and Journey
The Imholte Family

Gerald Monroe, Friend & Military Colleague

I was born and raised in Los Angeles and joined the Air Force at 19 years of age. Growing up in California, I never saw snow until I went to Wichita Falls, Texas... and, I got sick.

I served in the military 23 years, retired in 1993. I met Jeff at the Andrews Air Force Base. We were part of a flying squadron, together. We got along really well. We both lived on base and ended up traveling together a great deal. We worked together for five or six years, and during that time we ended up traveling lots of places and having a lot of fun. We were both young, then, but I can honestly say we did our jobs well... and, still had a lot of fun.

It's hard to sum Jeff up in one word, but if I had to, I would say: Friend. He is honest, truthful and has a great personality. Jeff was also what I'd call balanced—very much into his family and his job. The attributes that have likely been with him all his life is his smile, his personality and his positive attitude. Jeff's contribution to any organization he worked for was in his leadership. He was both a company man and a solid family man.

Everybody knew Jeff was great at sports—especially racquetball. Because of a motorcycle injury I sustained in Mexico, I was unable to play sports.

One memory of our time working together was a three- week Israel trip. The crew stayed in a really nice hotel. one night, someone knocked on the door, but when I opened it no one was there, then I looked up on the ceiling and there was Jeff, like Spiderman, attached to the ceiling. I couldn't believe it. But he was in great physical shape and loved to play gags on us. That was some trip. Everyone was walking around with Uzis, and machine guns... even the women.

Like Jeff, I flew with President Clinton and with First Lady Clinton up until I left in 1993. It was definitely a once in a lifetime experience. We met many famous celebrities and most of them were very nice. We met Sylvester Stallone, the President of the Philippines, the Duke and Duchess of Sussex, the Princess of Thailand, Joe Gibbs and Gerald McRaney. First Lady Barbara Bush used to give us gifts, Christmas cards and invited us to White House events.

By 1993, I had traveled to 72 countries. I'd say Brazil and Costa Rica were my favorite. But, by then I'd gotten tired of flying around the world and being away from my family. My family and I moved to Birmingham, Alabama in 1994, but Jeff and I still stay in touch, though we don't often see each other.

I'm excited that Jeff is running for Mayor of Niagara Falls. He will do a good job. He took us around and showed us his city when we worked together.

Glenn and Ronda Powell, Friends, Military Colleagues

I first met Jeff in 1995. I was working on the White House press plane then, and for this particular trip, the three flight attendants from AF 1 came over to visit on the press plane. Jeff was one of them. It was the first time I'd seen three black flight attendants on a trip together.

The things that I noticed about Jeff early on in our relationship were that he was very smart, a great judge of character, has impeccable integrity, is friendly and approachable and loyal. Jeff is much more of a family man, than a company man. He is the greatest father you ever want to see when it comes to his daughters.

Jeff doesn't seem as if he's changed at all, from the time we met in 1995. One thing I think has served him well throughout his life and career is his adaptability, and his honesty. If you ask Jeff anything, he won't sugarcoat his response, but won't hurt your feelings, either. Besides his love for racquetball, Jeff loves playing cards. I think playing cards took over as he started slowing down with racquetball.

One story from our years of travel was this one: We were on an overseas trip once and I was getting sleepy just as the attendants were about to serve us breakfast. I told Jeff that I wanted a pancake as big as my head. He literally went back to the kitchen and prepared this humongous pancake for me!

We had some amazing times traveling the world together. All the time that I've known Jeff, I have never seen him not smiling. If you are having a bad day, his smile will lift your spirits. When we met his family, we immediately saw where he gets his personality.

The running joke between myself and Jeff, is that I have spent more time with Jeff through our travels than I have spent with my wife, Ronda. Jeff and Ronda have a special friendship as well. Ronda calls Jeff her "second husband." He would call and check on her and the boys regularly when I was traveling. At Ronda's military retirement ceremony in 2007, Jeff presented her with a framed photo of himself, with hearts all around it. To this day, she has it hanging in her office.

Jeff and I remain close, and regularly check in with each other. We talk every couple of weeks. Ronda and I are very excited about Jeff running for mayor. He will make an excellent mayor. You have to be a people-person to be a mayor, and that fits Jeff perfectly. He is also a man of his word and will serve his community well in the capacity of mayor.

Buddy Rowe, Friend and Military Colleague

I'm originally from Arlington, Virginia. My mother was from Stanton, Virginia and for some reason people thought it was a cemetery. I met Jeff in the late 90's at the Andrews AF Base NCO Club. We quickly became friends playing Bid Whiz cards together. We became card partners over the years—playing our standard Thursday and Friday night card games at the NCO club, or at our partners' homes.

Over the years, our careers have overlapped quite a bit. I've worked with one caterer for over 20 years and would often tell Jeff he wasn't the only one working around important people, including catering events for Justice Sandra Day O'Connor and President Bush. I hired Jeff to work with me on several catering events. He was one of the few people who would agree to work a Christmas Eve party. This event was for a Catholic family in the area and they really loved Jeff. Of course, if you know Jeff, you know he can get along with anyone. I'm sure the fact that the job paid double overtime helped him make the decision to work it each year. He would go to Niagara Falls during many of his holidays but never for Christmas because he wanted to stay and work the Christmas Eve party.

While we don't see each other much now, I'll always consider him a good friend. What made Jeff stand out was how friendly and kind he was. He was always respectful to everyone. What stayed with you most was how funny he was. He always kept us laughing, telling little jokes.

The two memories of my friendship with Jeff that stick with me most are our Bid Whiz games and our tailgating weekends. My brother and I had Redskin season tickets; and our Bid Whiz partners would all come out on Sundays during football season and tailgate. Jeff was famous for his barbecued ribs. He used to brag about those ribs all the time. We always drilled him about the recipe, but Jeff wouldn't give it up. He said General Colin Powell used to ask him for the recipe, but he didn't give it to him, either.

Jeff had a buddy who played for the Redskins Band, and in the middle of or card games, Jeff would jump up and run up to the curb to make sure his friend saw him! We'd tease each other about our cooking. One of our buddies, when it was his time to cook, brought three different meats...but, forgot to cook the salmon. Jeff nicknamed him "Salmon." That was really a fun outing, and other people would sometimes come and join up with us. Jeff was the best cook. There were about seven of us who played bid whiz, and we'd be out there two hours after the game ended, still playing cards, joking and telling lies.

Jeff was also quite opinionated, but he would always give good advice because he was honest. He was devoted to his family. Everyone knew how much he loved his mother and his girls. Every year he would hold a cookout at his home and would invite his parents—though his mother and father weren't married, they were good friends. They would both be there every year for that cookout. That's how I figured out where Jeff got his sense of humor. His mother is a very funny person too. My two words to describe Jeff Elder: Funny Guy. The other thing is, Jeff is such a respectful guy. He treats everyone the same.

We were all very proud that Jeff's military career took him to high places. There weren't many people we knew whose job was flying on Air Force I, with the opportunity to meet Presidents and getting to know them. How many people get to do that?

As we all got older, I didn't see much change in Jeff. He was always the funny, down to earth guy who was usually the life of the party. But, over the last few years, he's talked more and more about running for Mayor of Niagara Falls. With his personality, I think Jeff would make a great mayor.

Bruce Shafer, Friend & Military Colleague

I met Jeff when I was working as a helicopter instructor pilot in Niagara Falls. It was around 1987. Niagara Airport had both a military side and a civilian side. I was part of the Army National Guard.

Jeff and I both loved racquetball and were both very competitive. I played it for 30 years. First time I saw Jeff, he was on the racquetball courts. I asked him if he wanted to play with me. He was young and thought he was going to wipe the courts with me. He could never beat me. Maybe 10-15 years later, after I had back surgery, we played each other and I won the first game, but he beat me the second round.

The last time I saw Jeff was in DC at his retirement celebration. When we had armed forces championship tournaments on the military base, we saw each other all the time. We also saw each other in Houston where they held the all-military championship tournaments.

When I moved to DC, I would run into Jeff on the Racquet ball court pretty regularly. When I went to Vietnam, I played racquet ball every day.

Jeff was what I'd call adaptable. That was his greatest contribution to an organization—adaptable to different situations and different people. He also brings enthusiasm and compassion for whatever he does.

Jeff was always both a company man and family man. He had a good balance of both. One of his most memorable traits is his sense of humor. He's a very funny guy. At one of the annual service banquets, Jeff and I was sitting across from each other. Someone was riding me about something, and when I got up to go to the bathroom, I reached in my pocket and pulled out my middle finger. Every time I saw him after that he'd say, "Don't go in your pocket."

Transformations? Jeff seems to just get better over the years. Something I think has probably defined Jeff his whole life: His ability to read people, and to get along with all kinds of people. Jeff will make a great Mayor!

My Lifetime of Memories in Photographs

Jeff and Dianna with President and Senator Clinton

Jeff and C-9 Flight Crew - McDonnell Douglas Flight

Jeff and Sharon Farmer Traveling the World

Jeff and Uncle Jeff on AF-1

Jeff in Search of Duct Tape

President Clinton, Jeffrey, Wanda Joell and Fellow Crew on AF-1
&

Jeff and Kevin on Overseas Travel - Mogadishu

Jeff's Overseas Travel - Check Point Charlie at the Berlin Wall

Jeffrey with Family and Friends

Jeffrey with His Parents

Munch's Family

Snook's family

Nat'l Military Racquetball Championship in Houston

Uncle Chief and Staff Sergeant Retirement

Jeff's first time golfing in Hawaii

Jeff Elder at Family Reunion in Niagara Falls

Index

James Brown 182-186

President Bush 112, 143, 144, 146,
    174, 193, 194, 205, 206, 209, 210, 257, 272

Rocky Carroll 190

President Carter 79

President Clinton 134, 136, 139, 140-142,
    153-155, 157-158, 161, 173, 182-190,
    192, 195-197, 257, 270, 278

Ann Compton 153, 195

Dale Earnhardt, Jr 192

Dale Earnhardt, Sr 192

Kenny G 190-192

Senator John Glenn 187

Cuba Gooding, Jr 186-187

Vice President Al Gore 264

Arsenio Hall 186

King Hussein 185

Peter Jennings 194-195

President Kennedy 256

Edward James Olmos 186

President Reagan 148

Carrol Shelby 193

Chris Tucker 187, 188

Brian Williams 194

Henry Winkler 185

Tiger Woods 183, 184